# The
# Channel Four Racing
# Guide to
# FORM and BETTING

# CHANNEL FOUR RACING GUIDES

edited by Sean Magee

*already published*

## RACECOURSES

with Derek Thompson

# The
# Channel Four Racing
# Guide to
# FORM and BETTING

with
**JIM McGRATH** and **JOHN McCRIRICK**
and members of the Channel Four Racing team

edited by
**SEAN MAGEE**

CHANNEL 4 BOOKS

First published in 1998 by Channel 4 Books, an imprint of Macmillan
Publishers Ltd, 25 Eccleston Place, London SW1W 9NF and Basingstoke

Associated companies throughout the world.

ISBN 0 7522 2197 3

9 8 7 6 5 4 3

A CIP catalogue record for this book is available from the British Library.

Commissioning Editor: Susanna Wadeson
Editors: Mari Roberts and Gillian Bromley
Design and production by Production Line
Printed by Mackays of Chatham plc, Chatham, Kent

This book accompanies the television series Channel Four Racing
made by Highflyer Productions for Channel 4.
Executive producers: John Fairley and Andrew Franklin

# Contents

# Illustrations

The racecard for the Scottish Champion Hurdle in the colour section is reproduced by kind permission of the *Racing Post*, as is the form on page 45.

All other photographs in the colour section are by George Selwyn.

The official form-book record of the 1998 Coral-Eclipse Stakes on page 47 is reproduced by kind permission of Raceform Ltd.

# Preface

Of all the different aspects of horse racing which the *Channel Four Racing Guides* seek to explain and illuminate, no area is more baffling to the uninitiated than the study of form and its natural corollary, having a bet.

But for most racing fans, working out which horse is going to win a race, and then putting your money where your opinion is, forms the sharp end of the whole sport, and the aim of the present *Guide* is to dispense basic information and guidance about form and betting on the simple basis that the more you know, the more effectively you will operate.

Much of the core information in the pages that follow has been developed from material first published in previous editions of *The Channel Four Book of Racing*; to this, Jim McGrath and John McCririck, Channel Four Racing's resident experts on form and betting respectively, add their particular insights, with the rest of the team chipping in on pages 9–10.

Thanks to all the presenters for their willing co-operation yet again, and to Andrew Franklin, Robert Cooper, Susanna Wadeson, Charlie Carman, Mari Roberts, George Selwyn, Gillian Bromley and Charlie Webster.

*Sean Magee*

# Words of wisdom from the Channel Four Racing team

**Alastair Down**

'I have two rules in betting, although my bank manager wishes it were more.

'First, never bet odds on, and secondly – and this should be branded on every racegoer's forehead – always check the Tote.

'If you were faced with two bookmakers' boards, with one offering 12–1 and the other 22–1, would you take the twelves? Yet by ignoring the Tote, punters often do just that, and those who persist in the habit deserve sectioning under the 1959 Mental Health Act.

'At big meetings especially, the Tote can offer tremendous value, particularly for horses from small yards or ridden by jockeys not in the first flush of fashion. So always check the old nanny goat – you're betting against your fellow punters, rather than the bookies, and sometimes the benefits can prove wallet-stuffingly spectacular.'

**John Francome**

'Watch horses, and follow the ones that really catch your eye: you can often do well by spotting a few improving three-year-olds and sticking with those. Always remember: you don't have to bet – so if you don't have a sound reason for betting, leave that race alone.'

**Graham Goode**

'Work out what you think the price of your selection should be, and only bet if the odds are better. Make betting a business by keeping a *true record of selections, then you can work out the profit on turnover. If you fritter for fun you'll fail in the long run.'*

### Lesley Graham

*'As the smallest of small-time punters – and certainly the smallest in the Channel Four Racing team! – I wouldn't pretend to have any great betting secret. But there's one piece of advice that every punter, big or small, must stick to religiously – never chase your losses.'*

### Simon Holt

*'Having faith in your own judgement is possibly the best advice I can give, particularly if you have been following horse racing for long enough to form an opinion and know when you have seen a good horse or witnessed a promising performance. Follow those instincts and you may be pleasantly surprised how often you are right.'*

### John Oaksey

*'Back in my riding days I was knocked out by a fall at Folkestone, and on my discharge from hospital – still suffering from the bang to the head – I staked hugely more than my usual bet in a £25 each-way Yankee: total stake £550. Three of the four came in, and had L. Piggott woken his ideas up on John Cherry in the Chester Cup I would have won over £20,000. As it was, I collected about £3,000, so I wasn't complaining too bitterly. Moral: bet only when suffering the effects of concussion.'*

### Brough Scott

*'Avoid stables that are out of form, and follow stables in form. Follow apprentices in form when they get hot. Back Kieren Fallon first time up on a ride outside Henry Cecil's yard: he's an improver of horses.'*

### Derek Thompson

*'Never bet odds on – it's as simple as that!'*

# Form –
# and how to use it

# Top of the form

## Jim McGrath

Solid study of the form book is essential for anyone who wants to take their betting seriously.

Just consider. The majority of races are won by the first or second favourite, and in many races those positions in the betting market will have been earned by form. Therefore the outcome of most races is predictable through careful study of the form, and the more time you can devote to that study, the better you'll bet.

There's no short cut, and to make proper use of the form and arrive at your decision by your own judgement – as opposed to following a newspaper tipster, or those know-alls on Channel Four Racing! – you must be prepared to devote time to the exercise.

During the Flat season there are so many meetings that virtually nobody can give due attention to every race. So, if your time is limited, it pays to concentrate on the better races, such events generally attracting good horses prepared by leading trainers and ridden by top jockeys. The form of these is more likely to prove reliable than that in lowlier races.

Form study is a vital element of picking winners, but always remember that it is not the only element, and if possible it needs to be combined with having a good look at the horses before a race – either on television or, ideally, in the flesh at the racecourse. Learn about the characteristics of individual horses, and assess their chances accordingly. That fine stayer Celeric, for example, bucks and kicks in the paddock when he's on really top form, but when he looks half asleep in the parade ring, take care: if he's not feeling well in himself, he won't run well. As for 1997 Derby winner Benny The Dip, John Gosden's charge would often work himself up into a lather before his races – we dubbed him Benny The Drip at Timeform – and when the lather dried off, his coat would look stary and patchy. But after a few runs it became apparent that his sweating did not affect his running and could safely be ignored, whereas the same symptoms in another horse could well signal a nervousness which would affect his performance adversely. Or take another example, Henry Cecil's colt Chester House. His early runs in 1998 displayed a distinct and very obvious correlation between his behaviour before a race and his performance in it. First time out at Kempton Park in April he behaved badly beforehand and ran badly; but as he learned to relax at the track, so his performances improved.

Get to know horses, and filter the brute facts of the form through what you can tell with your own eyes.

And the overriding moral: don't take form at face value.

Before we look at the main elements which make up the form picture, here's a handful of form and betting basics to have etched on to the first page of your form book . . .

- Know your horses: watch them closely, in particular the better ones, and not just when they're in action – knowing how they react before a race can be a definite help in predicting how they might perform in it. John Francome has a great eye for a horse and has proved time after time that study of the runners in the paddock really does pay. Remember his making Moonax his paddock 'eyecatcher' on Channel Four before the 1994 St Leger? The Barry Hills-trained colt did not appear to have the form to win the Classic, but he certainly had the looks – and obliged at 40–1. Franks would never, *ever*, back a horse if the animal did not look well.
- In the light of the above, try to leave placing your bet as late as possible. It's difficult to keep an eye on movements in the betting ring *and* get a good look at the horses, but if you're at the course you can gain a good impression of a

horse's well-being by studying him in the pre-parade ring – and then, if you like what you see, nip off to the ring to get on.

- Know the ground, and never forget that any horse unable to act effectively on the prevailing going is most unlikely to run to form.

- Always have regard for that age-old notion of 'horses for courses'. It makes a great deal of sense.

- Keep an eye out for horses moving up in distance if they have been noted as running on well towards the end of a shorter race. A horse which is running on does not lack stamina – in many cases, he needs a longer trip.

- Always be on the look-out for value. Exactly what constitutes 'value' for the punter is a subjective matter, but here's an example. Take a big field of handicappers. You look at the race with a view to picking the winner, and you find five horses with a real chance: it's difficult to divide them. If you take under 4–1 about any of those you need your head examining. But say one of them is on offer at 8–1 or more – win or lose, that's value. It's as simple as that: a horse represents value when the odds on offer are longer than you think reflect his chance. If you constantly back horses which are bad value, in the long term you will lose.

- If a horse runs badly and there is a good excuse, give it another chance. But if you don't know why it ran badly, leave it alone. You'll miss the odd winner, but you'll save yourself countless losers. Serious value can be had from forgiving one poor run when the reasons are not hard to find. Take 1998 Oaks winner Shahtoush. She ran a blinder when second to Cape Verdi in the One Thousand Guineas at Newmarket over one mile, a trip which her breeding suggested would be on the sharp side for her. She was then a big disappointment when only tenth in the Irish One Thousand Guineas. But that race came quite soon after her exertions in the Newmarket Classic; the ground at The Curragh was unsuitably fast for her; and she experienced traffic problems when trying to make her run. Forgiving sorts who knew she was a top-class filly – her run behind

Cape Verdi proved that – and was bred to be even better over the longer distance at Epsom had their faith rewarded when she swooped later under Mick Kinane to land the Oaks at 12–1.

- When in doubt, stay out! Successful betting is as much about not backing losers as about backing winners. And never chase your losses. There *is* always another day.

# The key factors

A three-horse race brings together three two-year-old colts – Angelic, Buttercup and Cowpat.

Each horse has run once before: Angelic and Buttercup in the same race, against Dunderhead (who is not running today), and Cowpat in a different race against Dunderhead. In their first race, over five furlongs on good going, Angelic and Buttercup carried the same weight and dead-heated to share second place, a length behind Dunderhead, who also carried the same weight. Today Angelic carries three pounds more than Buttercup and two pounds more than Cowpat. On the 'direct' form of the previous race against each other, Buttercup should this time finish in front of Angelic, as he now has a weight advantage. But 'collateral' form through another horse highlights the chance of Cowpat, as he beat Dunderhead a length at level weights when they met, whereas Angelic and Buttercup finished behind Dunderhead. Yes, but today's race is over seven furlongs, not five, and Angelic is bred for stamina. And today the going is heavy, not good, and Buttercup's dam liked soft going. Furthermore, Buttercup looked very burly in the parade ring before that race, and should be fitter today. Then again, Buttercup's trainer hasn't had a winner for six weeks . . .

Form is fact. The skill lies in its interpretation, and in weighing the comparative importance of the different elements which go to make up the complete form picture . . .

# DISTANCE OF THE RACE

Although some horses are genuinely versatile in terms of distance, most have an ideal trip or range of trips. What that ideal is will not necessarily be obvious until the horse has run a few times. For example, the four-year-old gelding Sandbaggedagain, trained by the irrepressible Mick Easterby, started the 1998 Flat season running over seven furlongs, though his only victory as a three-year-old had been over a mile and a half. After three unsuccessful outings at seven furlongs he was moved up to a mile and a quarter and started to find a little form; he stepped up to twelve furlongs on his next two outings and continued to run creditably without winning – then moved yet further up in distance to two miles and hit a winning vein, landing a handicap at Catterick before going on to take the Brown Jack Stakes at Ascot.

First indications of a horse's optimum distance lie with its breeding, as stamina, like speed, is hereditary. When it was announced in May 1998 that the filly Cape Verdi, having won the One Thousand Guineas over one mile, would be aimed at the Derby over one and a half miles, the first question was: did her breeding suggest she would stay? Her pedigree appeared to offer grounds for optimism. Her sire Caerleon had won the Prix du Jockey-Club over a mile and a half and had already sired a Derby winner in Generous; her dam Afrique Bleu Azur had won over eleven and a half furlongs in France, and was a daughter of Sagace, winner of the Prix de l'Arc de Triomphe over a mile and a half. On pedigree, it seemed reasonable to assume Cape Verdi would stay; but, as so often, it took the race to settle the point. At Epsom, the filly faded inside the final quarter mile – a telling indication that she had failed to last the trip.

The moral is simple. Racecourse performance is always the most reliable indicator of any aspect of form – and the corollary of that is that the more form a horse has, the fuller picture you build of him and the less you need to rely on guesswork and theory.

A word of warning, though: assessing that performance is not so simple. Several factors affect how far a particular performance testifies to a horse's stamina – the pace at which a race was run, the state of the going, the nature of the track – and these must be weighed up and interpreted. For instance, any horse which is staying on at the end of a truly run race over two miles at Newmarket in soft going may reasonably be assumed to 'get the trip' – that is, last out the full distance – whereas the winner of a slowly run race over two miles on firm going around a much tighter and flatter track such as Folkestone could not – on that evidence alone – be said to have the same degree of stamina.

The question of stamina is rarely clear-cut. Some experts think that the Derby course of a mile and a half can suit a horse which truly stays no more than a mile and a quarter, as more of it is downhill than uphill: Sir Ivor in 1968 is one example of a horse who won the Derby but whose performance elsewhere showed that his preferred trip was only one and a quarter miles.

**Jim McGrath says . . .**

*According to John Francome, who knows more about these matters than most, you can develop a horse's stamina, by teaching him to relax in his races and thus last longer. Do not equate stamina on the Flat with stamina over the same trip over jumps. A miler on the Flat will commonly get twice that trip when switched to racing over obstacles – where one factor is the brief respite which a horse gets from the act of jumping. Crossing twelve fences in a two-mile chase adds up to almost five seconds' relief from the arduous business of galloping, and two miles over jumps is much easier to get than two miles on the Flat. Another hint: don't take the form in two-mile 'bumpers' – National Hunt Flat Races – as an indication of equal merit with form over two miles on the Flat; many horses that run in – and win – bumpers do not truly stay that distance. Mary Reveley's Mellottie is a good example: he won two bumpers, over two miles and over thirteen furlongs, but on the Flat was in his element over a much shorter trip, winning the nine-furlong Cambridgeshire in 1991.*

# GOING

Although there is an old racing adage that a good horse can act on any going, the majority, even among the greatest, display a preference for a particular surface. Brigadier Gerard won seventeen of his eighteen races, but appeared ill at ease when racing on soft ground – though he still won on it.

---

Like so many aspects of racing, the state of the going is often discussed in a jargon which may seem baffling to newcomers. Here's a short glossary:

'top of the ground': firm, fast going
'bottomless': very heavy
'cut in the ground': on the soft side of good
'lively': on the firm side
'a sound surface': not too soft
'getting his toe in': on the soft side

---

Physical traits, too – conformation and action – will influence a probable suitability for extremes of ground. It is sometimes said that a horse with large feet will like the mud, on the grounds that a larger foot has more grip. As important as size alone is the horse's action, the way it moves. Watch as they canter to post: a horse with a 'round' action – one which brings its knees high in each stride – is likely to go well on soft or muddy going, while the animal with a more economical 'daisy-cutting' stride, where the feet seem to be lifted over the ground only just far enough to clear it, will probably find the soft less suitable, and act more effectively on fast ground. A horse that seems to 'float' elegantly over the ground on good going may well get stuck in the soft.

Clearly, if a horse appears to have a distinct preference for a particular state of going, its chances will be affected by the weather. Having the 'wrong' ground does not, of course, mean that the horse categorically will not win, but it does mean that he is unlikely to run to his best form.

In any race, no assessment of the runners' chances is complete that does not take into account the likely effect of the going. While most horses should be able to act effectively on good ground, when extremes occur – very hard or very heavy – always pay serious attention to horses who have won or run well on similar going in the past. A good recent example is Earth Summit, who won the 1998 Grand National on heavy going. He had won the Welsh National earlier the same season in similarly extreme conditions.

### Jim McGrath says . . .

*When Phil Bull, founder of Timeform and perhaps the greatest betting brain of the century, was interviewing prospective recruits for positions in the company, he would always put the question: What is the most important fact a punter needs to know before having a bet on a horse? The answer was: Will it act on the ground?*

*Like humans, horses are built in different ways, and their action – their manner of running – differs. For simple physical reasons, few are able to turn in the same level of performance on firm and on heavy. As a horse's racing record is built up, astute punters construct a picture of which going suits that horse ideally.*

*But it also pays to appreciate the difference between the same status of going at different courses, as this can influence how you assess a performance. Chepstow, for example, can get especially heavy when conditions are very wet, as can Aintree. The last few years have seen runnings of the Grand National in ground so heavy that only a few horses managed to get round: just six in 1994, Miinnehoma's year, and six again in 1998 when Earth Summit and Suny Bay drew well clear of their rivals in desperate conditions. Kempton Park is another course where conditions become very testing in heavy ground. When weighing up form in such circumstances, punters must take into account that fields will almost invariably return strung out – and that the distances separating the runners at the finish won't truly reflect their relative merits.*

*On the other hand, there is rarely genuinely soft going at Newmarket, as the course drains so well, and Doncaster doesn't often get seriously testing for Flat racing. A little course knowledge can definitely be of some help.*

*Incidentally, with modern watering systems providing a much more sophisticated form of irrigation than was available fifteen or so years ago, it is rarely the case that one side of a track will be genuinely faster than another, so take warily any pronouncements to that effect. There are exceptions, of course; the camber in the straight at Epsom Downs means that in very wet conditions the ground is usually worse on the inside – that is, lower – part of the track, and jockeys quite rightly tack across to the stands rail.*

*Whatever the horse, whatever the course, whatever the race: always take account of the state of the going.*

# CLASS

All form is relative to the class of the event in which it is recorded; so it is important to know the standard of each race you are contemplating when building up a picture of form. Fifth place in a Classic represents a much better performance than victory in a lowly race (though how far was the fifth horse behind the winner?). Information about the class of a race is easily gained from the detailed form in the racing press (see 'Sources of Information', page 43), which will give the prize money and level of the past race in question.

- On the Flat, there are six classifications, from Class A (Pattern and Listed races – that is, the cream of the year's events) down to Class G (selling races with small amounts of prize money, and apprentice and amateur races of similar value).
- Over jumps, there are seven ranks, from Class A (races run under the jumping Pattern) down to Class H (hunter-chases and National Hunt Flat Races – 'bumpers' – of low value).

You do not need to know the exact definition of each class, but you do need to be aware that form in a Class B race is likely to be of a significantly higher standard than form in a Class F race.

Whatever the race, the worth of the form becomes established as horses that took part appear again – either by (to use jargon) 'franking' or 'advertising' it or running poorly ('devaluing') it. Gradually a picture of the overall quality of the race is built up. Take, for example, the 1997 Vodafone Derby won by Benny The Dip. No one would dispute that this was a wonderfully exciting race, with the winner holding off the late surge of Silver Patriarch. But how, over the subsequent months, did the form hold up? Let's look at the bare bones of the subsequent form of each runner from the Derby until the end of 1997, listed in finishing order at Epsom:

| Horse | Runs | Wins |
|-------|------|------|
| 1 Benny The Dip | 3 | 0 |
| 2 Silver Patriarch | 3 | 1 (Group 1) |
| 3 Romanov | 4 | 1 (Group 3) |
| 4 Entrepreneur | 1 | 0 |
| 5 The Fly | 3 | 0 |
| 6 Fahris | 6 | 2 (Group 3, Listed) |
| 7 Symonds Inn | 0 | 0 |
| 8 Musalsal | 3 | 0 |
| 9 Bold Demand | 1 | 0 |
| 10 Cloudings | 0 | 0 |
| 11 Single Empire | 0 | 0 |
| 12 Crystal Hearted | 3 | 2 (Group 3, Group 2) |
| 13 Papua | 5 | 0 |

So between them the runners in the 1997 Derby ran on thirty-two more occasions that year, managing to win six times, with just a single Group One win (Silver Patriarch in the St Leger). What does that suggest to you about the overall quality of that Derby field?

Hindsight is a great factor in the study of form: make use of it. Go through the previous races of each day's winners and mark them off: the form of a heavily marked event is clearly working out well. Such a trend may point you towards horses yet to race. If the form is standing up, those horses are worth looking for.

**Jim McGrath says . . .**

*The class of a race can be gauged by how many horses go on from it to show improvement – measured, for example, through their official handicap ratings – and can only be gained through hindsight and a good deal of cross-referencing. If you are trying to assess the class of a maiden race where the runners have no previous form, your immediate pointer will be the time of the race, compared with others on the day. Subsequently you will be able to go on the later performances of the runners.*

*Don't jump to conclusions too quickly about the class of a race. The fact that City Honours, narrowly beaten by High-Rise in the 1998 Derby, and Sunshine Street, fourth at Epsom, both ran disappointingly on their next appearance in the Irish Derby might suggest that the class of the Epsom race will not bear close scrutiny. Whether or not that turns out to be the case in the fullness of time, the Irish Derby comes soon after Epsom and both horses were almost certainly feeling the effects of their exertions in the English Classic.*

*Moral: take class seriously but tread warily until there's enough evidence.*

# TIME

The study and use of race times can be immensely complicated, and most casual punters have only a vague notion of how important an element of form the matter of time can be, generally leaving it to the time experts in the racing press to tell them what is significant.

Compared with human athletes, horses have not, as a whole, got much faster over the last fifty years. But though record times themselves are not considered especially important, the comparison of the times that different horses take to win different races over the same course can be very significant – it is worth noting that many of the top professional backers consider the study of race times one of the most significant weapons in their battle against the bookmakers – and it was to facilitate such comparisons that the concept of the standard time was introduced. The standard time on the Flat is a time for each distance at each course adjusted to a horse carrying nine stone on good or firm ground, and is calculated by taking the average of the ten fastest runnings. Courses vary hugely, as standard times reflect. At the beginning of 1998 the Raceform standard time over five furlongs at Epsom was 54.5 seconds; at Sandown Park, with its stiff uphill finish, the standard time for the same trip was 1 minute 0.7 seconds. The time of the winning horse will be given in relation to standard, 'above' meaning slower than standard, 'below' faster.

The advantage of race times is that they constitute a completely objective body of evidence which can be used to compare the abilities of horses who have never raced against each other. However, remember that the evidence of the clock must be tempered by other considerations: was the race run at a true pace, was it run at the end of a day when heavy rain throughout the programme might have changed the going, was the winner pushed out to the line or was he easing up? As with every aspect of form, all these details need to be factored in – which brings us back to the experts in the racing papers and form services, who do the maths and come up with ratings based on time.

**Jim McGrath says . . .**

*For the average everyday punter my advice as far as the time of races is concerned is straightforward: either leave it alone completely, or leave it to the experts. Stick to what you are comfortable with – and if you're comfortable with the use of adjusted race times, you're probably an expert anyway!*

*If you're going to get involved in the analysis of time, do it thoroughly. Basically, time students – who may use differing methods towards the same end – seek to establish a standard against which each individual performance on any given racing day may be measured; in this way each day's racing, race by race, provides a guide, a feel for that particular day which provides yet another piece in the mosaic of form.*

*A method for establishing a standard for a single day's racing is as follows:*

*Divide the number of furlongs of each race into 100, and express this as pounds: thus each furlong in a five-furlong race is worth twenty pounds, in a one-mile race twelve and a half pounds, in a two-mile race six and a quarter pounds. Say a race over each distance that day is won by a five-year-old carrying ten stone, and each records a time one second better than standard for that course, which is the most meritorious performance, in terms of time? Answer: the winner of the two-mile race, who has posted a result nearly fourteen pounds better than the five-furlong winner (twenty less six and a quarter equals nearly fourteen). Our example, of course, is simplistic – deliberately so; as in open-aged races, times have to be adjusted to the Weight-for-Age scale (see page 122), and so on and so on. The advice has to be: either know what you're doing, or steer clear!*

# COURSE

You can do a lot worse than follow the notion of 'horses for courses' when trying to pick a winner, especially on notoriously quirky tracks such as Chester, Epsom or Windsor. Any horse running on a course where it has won before is worthy of consideration, for it is clearly able to act effectively on that track; exactly how much importance you attach to such evidence depends on both horse and course. Remember, too, that while all British racecourses are different, many have some aspects in common, and it pays to know something of the nature of each track: is it right-handed or left-handed, is it flat or undulating, galloping or tight? (You can find this information in the *Channel Four Racing Guide to Racecourses*.) By familiarising yourself with the intricacies, you will become better equipped to judge whether the horse you saw scoot home in a three-mile chase at Kempton is likely to find the same trip at Cheltenham equally suitable.

---

Five horses for five courses

- Tempering has won twenty-two races on the all-weather track at Southwell
- Rapporteur won nineteen times at Lingfield Park – fourteen times on the all-weather track
- Suluk won eighteen races at Southwell (all-weather again)
- Manhattan Boy won fourteen races at Plumpton
- Rapid Lad won twelve races at Beverley

---

**Jim McGrath says . . .**

*The idea of horses for courses is based on a very simple notion, but as with so many of these main elements of the form picture, it pays to take the idea a bit further and get to know particular characteristics of individual courses. For example, it's no coincidence that three in* the list of some well-known horses for courses opposite are all-weather specialists. Some horses specialise on the artificial surfaces, and since there are so few tracks for them to run on, consistent winners are bound to run up big totals at those tracks. But be aware that the two surfaces used for all-weather racing are significantly different, and very few horses act as well on the one as on the other. Equitrack, in use at Lingfield Park, is a far quicker surface than the Fibresand at Southwell and Wolverhampton, and much more conducive to pace. Fibresand is a much more demanding surface.

Naturally the quirkier courses are more likely to produce course specialists, but you must also bear in mind that form at such tracks should not necessarily be taken at face value when a horse is running elsewhere. Chester form often does not work out elsewhere, for a variety of reasons. One is that the very tight shape of the course makes the draw such a crucial element there. For instance, Blundell Lane won a six-furlong handicap at the May meeting from the hugely favoured number 1 draw, breaking fast to scorch round and win easily in a typical Chester performance. Next time out at Newmarket, again over six furlongs, there was no such draw advantage, and though he again broke smartly he failed to get home, fading to finish down the field.

It also seems to be the case that Chester favours what might be termed 'dodgy' horses, the type of animal whose attention wanders on the wide expanses of Newmarket but whose interest is engaged by the hurly-burly of racing round the Roodeye. Another characteristic of Chester is that finishing distances get exaggerated, and this should be taken into account when assessing Chester form. Over jumps, a similar situation applies on the Mildmay Course at Aintree. What links that course with Chester is that at both places races tend to be run at a very fast pace – which gets the field well strung out at the finish.

Do not assume that stamina necessarily counts for less at a tight track. Again take Chester as an example: it may be barely a mile round, but trainer Barry Hills for one is convinced that a Chester horse really needs to get the trip – and Barry's record at the course suggests that he knows what he's talking about.

Over jumps, take into account the known severity of steeplechase fences at a particular course. At Fontwell the fences are considered *soft, so the form of a horse running well there and going on to Newbury, where the fences are much stiffer, might be treated with caution.*

*In any case, don't get carried away by the sheer logic of the idea of horse for courses. Remember that horses lose as well as win at their favourite courses!*

# TRAINER AND JOCKEY

In 1998 Henry Cecil sent out nine consecutive winners, and Clive Brittain seventy-one consecutive losers. When a stable is on a roll, it pays to follow it; the trick, of course, is cottoning on to this when the yard is coming to the boil, not when the winning streak is petering out. The racing press gives detailed information about which trainers and jockeys are in good form, and about which have especially good records at particular courses, and these statistics can be invaluable. Conversely, when a stable has hit a thin patch, you would be well advised to be very wary of its runners until its form picks up – as supporters of David Nicholson's powerful jumping yard discovered to their cost at Cheltenham in March 1998: The Duke's stable was in the doldrums at the time, and had no Festival winners. Poor form by a particular yard is often caused by a virus affecting the horses, which does not become apparent until they run: in these circumstances it is very difficult to support a horse sent out by that trainer with any confidence, and whatever the attractions of his form on paper, the punter does best to be wary, bearing in mind the theory that it is better to miss a winner than back a loser – though while the advice is incontrovertible on the grounds that it costs you nothing in monetary terms to see the horse you were going to back romp home, the emotional anguish can be severe . . .

Jockeys, too, have purple patches, and a winning run can do wonders for a rider's confidence, lending the pilot an assurance that flows down the reins and galvanises the horse. Always pay attention to a jockey hitting a seam of form. And note who has ridden a horse in previous races: if for the current race Eddery or Dettori is taking the ride on a runner usually partnered by an apprentice or a lesser-known rider, that could be significant. Look out, too, for a top jockey who has gone to an obscure meeting to ride for an unfashionable stable: he will not have done so simply for the pleasure of a drive in the country. And in particular, pay heed to which jockeys do noticeably well at those tracks considered particularly difficult to ride – Epsom, say, or Bath or Catterick. The papers will give you a list of top jockeys there over the last few years, and these lists always repay close study.

**Jim McGrath says . . .**

*Following in-form trainers and avoiding out-of-form yards can enhance the success of your betting considerably, both by pointing you towards winners and by helping you steer clear of losers. Of course, it can never work out completely – an out-of-form stable can still send out the odd winner – but it pays to keep a close eye on a trainer's form.*

*Pay particular attention to the big yards – which have such fire-power that they should be having winners all the time – and to notable small yards.*

*Try to gauge the crucial period: catch trainers as they come out of the doldrums, and be quickly aware that they are going back in. A fairly obvious warning sign is when a big yard sends out a couple of beaten favourites.*

# DRAW

In races on the Flat over less than a mile, the draw – the allocation of each runner to the numbered stall from which it will start – can have a crucial effect on a horse's chance, although over longer distances its influence is usually considerably less. The effect of the draw is much more marked at some courses than others: at certain courses in some conditions a horse with a particular draw might have a negligible chance – in which case, while you might not want to back it that time, a prominent run is possibly more meritorious than it appears at face value. So always note the draw in races which are building up the form picture, for it will have a bearing on how you interpret the result.

---

Anticipation that the draw would prove a major factor in the outcome of the 1998 Vodafone Stewards' Cup at Goodwood was borne out. Of the twenty-nine runners,

- the winner Superior Premium was drawn 28
- the runner-up Ansellman was drawn 25
- the third, Eastern Purple, was drawn 29
- the fourth, Nigrasine, was drawn 23

Canny punters combining the highest five numbers in the draw in the inaugural Tote Trifecta bet (see page 71) were amply rewarded.

---

**Jim McGrath says . . .**

*Know your courses, and study the plan of the course: if the runners go into a bend shortly after the start, the draw is likely to be a crucial factor, with those drawn on the inside at an advantage.*

*Be aware of how going can affect the draw. In straight races at Newcastle or Thirsk, for example, high numbers (stands rail) are favoured – unless the going is soft, when the advantage rests with the low numbers (far rail). In neither case is a draw in the middle of a large field likely to be an advantage.*

# THE BETTING MARKET

For each horse taking part in a race, the form published in the racing press will include a summary of how the odds offered about that runner altered between the time betting opened on the event and the start of the race. This information can be highly revealing, for a horse whose odds shorten is being backed, while one whose odds lengthen is attracting less money – and these indications about confidence behind a horse, or the lack of it, constitute another piece in the form mosaic.

**Jim McGrath says . . .**

*Always assess betting moves within the context of the course market. A major move at a big meeting – the Cheltenham Festival, say, or Royal Ascot – is much more significant than at a small meeting, where crowds are sparse and it takes very little off-course money to manipulate the market.*

*Be wary of letting market moves put you off a selection you've made on grounds of form, the appearance of the horse, etc., and only be dissuaded from your original choice if the vibes in the betting ring are so bad they can't be ignored. When Sir Michael Stoute's filly Confidante ran at Ascot on the Saturday following the Royal Meeting in 1998 she looked sure to start favourite: she had a clear chance on form and had been recommended by two of the major tipping services. But after opening at 3–1 favourite in the course betting she drifted out to her starting price of 9–2, an obvious sign that there was little confidence behind her chance. Sure enough, she ran poorly.*

# THE RUNNING OF THE RACE

A key element in the form picture of any horse is a brief description of how it ran in each race recorded. Was it running on at the finish (in which case it has no stamina problems, and might need a longer trip)? Was it able to accelerate? Did it make the pace, or come from last to first? Did it encounter problems in running which might explain an otherwise unexpectedly poor finishing position? The comments given in the form are for the most part bald and factual – the closest the writers ever get to overt enthusiasm is 'won easily' – but from the depressingly straightforward 'always behind, tailed off' or 'never near enough to challenge' to the equally straightforward 'never headed', these laconic comments will tell you a lot about the way the horse fared. A particular pointer to future performance can be 'ran on well'; win or lose, the horse described thus was still racing right up to the line.

**Jim McGrath says . . .**

*By studying how past races were run, you will build up a picture of the running styles of individuals – whether a horse is a front-runner or suited by being held up – which will enable you to anticipate how the present race will be run. This can be a very important aspect of form.*

*Why? Because each horse's style of running is a crucial aspect of its form profile. Say there are several front-runners in a race: they might cut each other's throats and allow a horse who needs to be held up to come through close home. If there is no apparent pacemaker, is there a runner who can benefit from enterprising jockeyship? Some horses, reliable as they may be, simply feel they have done enough once hitting the front and start to doss. Therefore it would do nothing for their chances if they were forced to make the pace. Others are more versatile.*

*Again the moral is: get to know your horses.*

# TIME SINCE LAST RACE

Put bluntly, recent form is the best form; indeed, many shrewd punters will not back a horse when its form, however good, dates from a period too long before the current race. But sometimes old form is all one has – notably, of course, on a horse's seasonal debut. With horses that race for season after season, it pays to be aware of whether they tend to need a run or two to get to their top form, or whether they are usually ready to do themselves justice first time out.

Most newspapers print alongside each runner in each event the number of days since the horse last raced: a horse that has not run for a very long time could well be rusty and need this race to make it fit. But punters who turned against Derby runners Lammtarra in 1995 and Shaamit in 1996 on the grounds that they had not had a previous race that season would have had cause to rue their prejudice: Lammtarra won the premier Classic at 14–1, and Shaamit at 12–1.

**Jim McGrath says . . .**

*Whether a long lay-off reflects adversely on a horse's chance depends entirely on the horse: some need time between their races, some thrive on running frequently.*

*Take particular note of sprinters: they can hit 'seams' of form in which they run frequently and can hold their form very well for several races over a short period of time. Once a good handicap sprinter gets into that seam, follow him. During such a seam the horse may be running off his old official handicap mark (see page 41) before being reassessed, but don't get too fussy over ratings: if the horse is fit and well and running at the top of his form, and if he has the ideal ground, a pound or two in weight is not going to make much difference.*

# WEIGHT

You've studied everything about the runners, and picked your fancy: he's done a good time over this distance, he loves the course, the going is just right for him, his jockey is flying, his trainer can do no wrong – but if he's carrying two stone more than the best of his rivals, you'd have to think again.

In the Classics, all horses carry the same weight (except for an allowance to fillies in the Two Thousand Guineas, Derby and St Leger), so weight is not an element in assessing the likely outcome. The same is true of the premier National Hunt races. But in many other races there are discrepancies in the weights carried that must be taken into account. In 'weight-for-age' races, these discrepancies are calculated to counterbalance the advantage that a more mature horse will have over a younger rival: the Weight-for-Age Scale (pages 122–5) lays down the officially designated differences for horses of different ages over different distances at different times of the year, and naturally the effect of weight variations will not be the same at all distances: if a horse is beaten a neck in a five-furlong sprint he will theoretically dead-heat with his conqueror next time they meet if it carries one pound less weight; in a three-mile steeplechase a pound is generally regarded as worth a length.

The effect of weight is most marked, of course, in handicaps: races in which the runners are allotted different weights to render their chances theoretically equal. Naturally, handicapping is an inexact activity, and you need to be aware of this when assessing the performance of runners in this type of event: more credence can be given to the distances separating the first three or four home than the distances between the stragglers. Often, too, a horse will win easily but not by very far: alert observers will make due allowances.

Remember that a horse running 'out of the handicap' does not have a good chance at the weights. A horse is 'out of the handicap' if under the terms of that race he has to carry a weight greater than he was originally allotted in relation to the horse carrying the highest weight in the race. For example, Samlee, who finished third in the 1998 Grand National carrying the minimum weight of ten stone, should according to the 'long handicap' – the list of weights framed with regard only to the horses' previous performances, without regard to the minimum weight stipulated in the race conditions – have carried only nine stone four pounds. He was thus at a ten-pound disadvantage with those runners (a mere eight out of the field of thirty-nine) who were running on their 'true' handicap mark.

A brief rule of thumb for relating weight to finishing distances is:

Flat
- 5 furlongs to 7 furlongs: 3 pounds per length
- 1 mile to 11 furlongs: 2 pounds per length
- 1½ miles to 2 miles: 1½ pounds per length
- over 2 miles: 1 pound per length

National Hunt
- 1 pound per length (though make downward adjustments for extreme distances)

### Jim McGrath says . . .

*The weight which a horse carries is naturally very important, but don't try to treat weight with slide-rule precision: it's just one of a number of factors. Be aware of what the weight carried in a handicap indicates: is the horse improving or declining?*

*To ordinary punters, the Weight-for-Age scale is one of the more boring aspects of form, but any punter should be aware of what it means and should have access to it (which is why we've given it to you on pages 122–5). The Weight-for-Age scale is a tried and tested method of bringing generations together, an official assessment of how the average young horse will catch up on his elders in terms of maturity as the months and years pass. The knack with, say, an improving three-year-old running against older horses is to catch him when he starts to thrive, find his ideal distance, and so on – and so gets his act together that he defies the differences laid down in the scale and is capable of beating his elders.*

*The really great three-year-olds don't need the Weight-for-Age scale anyway. No one is suggesting that 1991 Derby winner Generous would not have won that year's King George against his elders had he met them on level weights, but generally the current scale is a successful method of allowing respective generations to race competitively.*

# REFINEMENTS

As well as these key elements which no student of form can omit from the calculations, there are other factors which can usefully be put into the melting pot.

## First-time blinkers

The purpose of fitting blinkers on a horse for a race is to get him to concentrate on the business in hand by focusing his sight to the front, rather than allowing him to be distracted by goings-on in his lateral field of vision. Some horses become wise to this ploy and get used to the blinkers, thus minimising their effect, so the first run wearing them can produce a significant improvement in form. Don't think of blinkers as an indication of an irresolute nature – Dream Well wore blinkers in 1998, and the way he won the Prix du Jockey-Club and Irish Derby did not suggest any lack of conviction; and the manner in which the blinkered Earth Summit won the 1998 Grand National in desperate going was evidence of the doughtiest spirit.

**Jim McGrath says . . .**

*Be more wary of first-time blinkers when fitted to stayers. With sprinters, they often give a horse an edge – that ability really to focus on the race – which can make all the difference.*

## Distance travelled to racecourse

On the basis that, say, an inmate of Martin Pipe's yard making the 377-mile journey from his stable in Nicholashayne in Devon to the racecourse at Ayr would not be doing so for a relaxing drive up the motorway, some form experts pay great attention to horses who have been sent a significantly long way to race. The *Racing Post* provides a list of such runners for each day.

**Jim McGrath says . . .**

*Everyone wants to go to the big meetings of the year, so whether a horse has travelled a long way to get to Cheltenham in March is unlikely to be of great significance. But pay special attention to horses driven extreme distances to lesser meetings – especially from lesser yards. If John Dunlop sends a horse from Arundel to Pontefract, the fact is unlikely to go unnoticed by punters. But if a small trainer sends a horse on a very long journey to run, that could be the opportunity for a value bet.*

## First run for a new trainer

Many horses benefit from a change of scene, and a move from one trainer to another can be significant. Whether it heralds a marked improvement in performance tends to depend on who he's left and who he's joined!

\*

Form is fact – a mass of fact. What you have to do is learn how to read, interpret and use all the strands in that mass of fact, and to add to it the magic extra ingredient of your own opinion. Remember that form only takes you up to the last performance; to come to your final assessment of the horses' chances, it must be accompanied by your judgement of the runners' condition before the race.

And don't forget that the same mass of fact is also available to the bookmakers!

# Ratings

Every horse in training, once it has run often enough to be assessed, is given an official rating by the handicappers of the British Horseracing Board, in the range

- on the Flat: 0–140;
- over jumps: 0–175.

Each point on this scale is equivalent to a pound in weight: that is, Horse A, rated 121, is deemed to be one pound 'better' than Horse B, rated 120, which in turn means that were they to race against one another with Horse A carrying nine stone two pounds and Horse B carrying nine stone one pound, they should theoretically dead-heat.

The official rating is revised every week, going up or down or staying the same depending both on how the horse has performed and on whether a race in which he has run has proved to be of better quality than originally considered. So should a horse win off a particular rating, or 'mark', and there is time to run again before he is rehandicapped – that is, his official rating is revised – connections may well be tempted to give him another race during that period if a suitable opportunity arises. In some cases a penalty – an additional weight to be carried if the horse has won a race since the last revision – will apply to take account of the improvement not yet reflected in the official ratings.

So when you hear a Channel Four pundit refer to a horse having 'won off 99', and relating that to his current mark, he or she is referring to the horse's official rating. And reference to a '0–90 handicap' means a handicap for horses rated no higher than 90.

As an example of how official ratings are revised to reflect improvement in a horse, consider the case of Lady Rockstar, the Mick Ryan-trained filly whose sequence of eight wins in a row in less than five weeks was a feature of the early part of the 1998 Flat season. When she started her winning run she was rated a very lowly 41, and then . . .

| | |
|---|---|
| 28 May | won at Ayr off 41 |
| 3 June | won at Folkestone off 46 |
| 5 June | won at Haydock, still off 46 |
| 11 June | won at Yarmouth off 53 |
| 17 June | won at Nottingham off 62 |
| 22 June | won at Windsor off 70 |
| 26 June | won at Folkestone off 71 |
| 29 June | won at Windsor off 73 |
| 8 July | unplaced at Newmarket off 84 |

. . . and her rating for future races had been increased to 89 by the time of that Newmarket appearance.

Apart from the official BHB ratings, some newspapers publish their own private handicaps; these will be broadly similar to the official list but may include some significantly different assessments, according to how each individual pundit interprets the form.

**Jim McGrath says . . .**

*Sprinters tend to have a better chance of keeping one step ahead of the official handicapper because they can run more often than middle-distance horses or stayers, and thus can get in another run – sometimes more than one – at their old mark before they're reassessed.*

# Sources of information

The official form book, published by Raceform on behalf of the British Horseracing Board and available in weekly or twice-weekly instalments, provides extensive details of every race run in Great Britain as well as the major races overseas. (See pages 46–7.)

Beyond the official form book, there are several sources of information, some more elaborate than others.

The *Racing Post* – since the demise of the *Sporting Life* in May 1998, the only daily racing newspaper in Britain – includes very extensive and sophisticated statistics. A detailed run-down of the form of every runner in every race is laid out, along with expert interpretation of that form. Also provided in a mind-boggling array of data are such additional details as the *Post*'s own ratings, and how these relate to the official ratings; trainers' and jockeys' records; statistics regarding the performance of favourites at each of the day's tracks; which horses have travelled furthest to the meetings; and lots more.

The sports pages of the national daily papers print the day's racing programmes, and some offer brief form summaries and related information, while racegoers are usually provided with a three-line form summary of each runner in the racecard. But for specialist information on a daily basis you have to consult the *Racing Post* – or, on Saturdays, the *Post*'s new opposition in the form of *Raceform on Saturday*, which first hit the nation's news stands on 25 July 1998, the day when Swain won the King George VI and Queen Elizabeth Diamond Stakes at Ascot for the second time.

Best-known of the private companies that dispense information about racing form is Timeform, based at Halifax in Yorkshire. Now the largest concern in the world devoted to the publication of form, Timeform was founded by the late Phil Bull (see page 100), a visionary whose strictly logical approach to the business of betting on racehorses transformed the nature of the battlefield on which punter takes on bookmaker.

Timeform produces a wide variety of publications, notably the annuals *Racehorses* (which lists and discusses every runner on the Flat) and *Chasers and Hurdlers* (for jumpers), and the daily Timeform Racecard, which provides detailed runner-by-runner analysis of every race at every meeting, and rates the chances of each horse according to Timeform's own ratings. (A rating accompanied by the dreaded 'Timeform squiggle' indicates a horse of unreliable temperament.)

If you have neither the time nor the inclination to sift the data yourself or follow the guidance of newspaper form experts, you can buy the services – and the inside information – of those whose advertisements for telephone tipping lines pepper the pages of the racing press. But it's so much more satisfying to work it all out on your own.

The form of Swain in the *Racing Post* on the morning of the King George VI and Queen Elizabeth Diamond Stakes, 25 July 1998.

Swain is a bay horse by the stallion Nashwan out of the mare Love Smitten, who herself is by the stallion Key To The Mint. His breeding details are followed by his placings in seventeen career runs over four seasons, the divisions between one year and another being marked by '/', the most recent division (i.e. between 1997 and 1998) being marked by '-': thus he has, in the season to date, run second, second and third.

He is trained by Saeed Bin Suroor, is six years old, and is due to carry nine stone seven pounds.

Swain's official rating is 127, and in his seventeen starts he has scored six victories, finished second four times and third five times. His win and place prize money to date is £1,472,012.

Beneath this information comes a list of those six victories, starting with the most recent – which happens to have been in the King George the previous year: in July 1997 he won at Ascot a one mile four furlong Grade A Group One event run on soft going, which netted his connections £294,600. Before that he had won a Group Three event at Longchamp in September 1996, and so on . . .

Then come details of Swain's last six outings, again in reverse order. On 19 June he had finished third at Ascot in a Grade A, Group Two race worth £77,050 to the winner. Seven horses had run in that race, the going was good to soft, and the time of 2 minutes 34.79 seconds was 2.79 seconds slower than standard. The race had been won by Posidonas, a six-year-old carrying eight stone nine pounds, ridden by Pat Eddery, drawn 7 and starting at 15–2. Germano was second and Swain, ridden by Frankie Dettori, drawn 5 and starting 6–5 on favourite, third. His run is described, followed by his rating with Postmark (PM 120), the *Post*'s own handicap, and his score on the paper's Top Speed scale (TS 102). In the betting for that race he had opened at 5–4 on and touched even money and 11–10 before reverting to odds-on.

The distances show that Swain finished two lengths behind the winner, and the new Postmark ratings for the first three in that race will be 118, 117 and 120.

To look at Swain's form in his race before that, consult the form entry for another of the King George runners who had beaten him on that occasion – Silver Patriarch.

## Swain

b h Nashwan - Love Smitten (Key To The Mint)
Placings: 1113/312143/2137-223

**Saeed Bin Suroor**      **6**    **9-7**

OR127

| | | Starts | 1st | 2nd | 3rd | Win & Pl |
|---|---|---|---|---|---|---|
| | | 17 | 6 | 4 | 5 | £1,472,012 |
| 7/97 | Asct | 1m4f A Gp1 soft | | | | £294,600 |
| 9/96 | Lonc | 1m4f Gp3 good | | | | £28,986 |
| 6/96 | Epsm | 1m4f A Gp1 good | | | | £106,560 |
| 8/95 | Deau | 1m4½f Gp2 good | | | | £59,880 |
| 8/95 | Deau | 1m4½f good | | | | £16,766 |
| 6/95 | StCl | 1m6f Gp3 3yo good | | | | £26,347 |
| | | | | Total win prize-money | | £533,139 |

**19 Jun Ascot 1m4f**      A Gp2 £77,050
7 ran   GD-SFT      Time 2m 34.79s (slw 2.79s)
1 Posidonas 6 8-9 .................Pat Eddery ⁷ 15/2
2 Germano 5 8-9 .........................M Roberts ⁴ 8/1
3 SWAIN 6 9-0 ............................L Dettori ⁵ 5/6F
*held up, led over 2f out, ridden over 1f out, headed inside final furlong, not quicken*
  [PM120 TS102]     [op 4/5 tchd Evs & 11/10]
Dist: ½-1½-8-1¾-shd    RACE PM: 118/117/120

**5 Jun Epsom 1m4f**      A Gp1 £106,125
second, see **SILVER PATRIARCH**

**28 Mar Nad Al Sheba 1m2f**    Gp1 £1,463,415
9 ran   FAST      Time 2m 4.29s
1 Silver Charm 4 9-0 .........................G Stevens
2 SWAIN 6 9-0 ...............................M J Kinane
*always in touch, 4th straight, strong challenge final furlong, just failed* [PM128]
3 Loup Sauvage 4 9-0 .........................O Peslier
Dist: shd-2½-shd-15-5    RACE PM: 128/128/123

**5 Oct 97 Longchamp 1m4f**     Gp1 £448,934
18 ran   GD-FM      Time 2m 24.60s
1 Peintre Celebre 3 8-11 .........O Peslier ² 22/10F
2 Pilsudski 5 9-5 ...................M J Kinane ¹⁵ 38/10
3 Borgia 3 8-8 .........................K Fallon ¹ 162/10
7 SWAIN 5 9-5 .........................L Dettori ¹³ 94/10
*always prominent, 3rd straight, every chance well over 1f out, hard ridden & one pace final furlong btn 8 lengths* [PM123 TS128]
Dist: 5-2½-shd-shd-snk RACE PM: 136+/128/120

**18 Sep 97 Newbury 1m3f**     A List £31,434
5 ran   GD-FM      Time 2m 18.97s (fst 1.03s)
1 Posidonas 5 9-2 .........................T Quinn ⁵ 8/1
2 Arabian Story 4 9-2 ...................K Fallon ³ 11/2
3 SWAIN 5 9-9 ...........................L Dettori ¹ 1/2F
*held up in rear, headway over 3f out, led over 1f out until inside final furlong, ran on*
  [PM123 TS100]     [ tchd 8/15 & 4/9]
Dist: shd-shd-3½-6     RACE PM: 104/103/110

**26 Jul 97 Ascot 1m4f**      A Gp1 £294,600
8 ran   SOFT      Time 2m 36.45s (slw 4.45s)
1 SWAIN 5 9-7 ..............................J Reid ⁵ 16/1
*held up, led over 2f out, edged right over 1f out, driven out* [PM130 TS127] [op 14/1 tchd 20/1]
2 Pilsudski 5 9-7 .........................M J Kinane ⁶ 6/1
3 Helissio 4 9-7 ...............C Asmussen ² 11/10F
Dist: 1-1¼-2½-4-5     RACE PM: 130/128/127

*Opposite:* The official form book record of the Coral-Eclipse Stakes at Sandown Park on 4 July 1998 – all you could possibly want to know about that race, bar the height which Frankie Dettori reached when leaping off the winner Daylami . . .

The description is headed by the reference number of the race (2550) followed by race name (Coral-Eclipse Stakes), Pattern standing (Group One), age range (three-year-olds and upwards) and ranking (Class A).

The race was due to start at 4.05 and actually started at 4.06, over a distance of one mile two furlongs and seven yards. Value to the owner of the winner was £147,600, to the second £55,100, third £26,350, fourth £11,350. The starting stalls were positioned 'high' – that is, towards where the high numbers in the draw start: in the case of a ten-furlong race at Sandown Park, that means on the inner rail. 'GOING minus 0.14 sec per fur (G)' indicates that the going was good ('(G)') and that the Raceform Going Allowance for that race was 0.14 seconds per furlong – that is, the state of the going meant that the winner could be expected to take 1.4 seconds (ten furlongs times 0.14) longer than standard time for that distance.

The winner Daylami had last run in race number 2011 and finished third. Daylami was foaled in Ireland, is trained by Saeed Bin Suroor, is four years old and carried nine stone seven pounds; he was ridden by Frankie Dettori and drawn 5. There then follows the bare description of his running in the race: he chased the leader for the first furlong, chased the leader again over two furlongs from the finish, took the lead over one furlong from the finish, was hard ridden and ran on well.

Daylami finished first (1); his starting price was 6–4 favourite. His Raceform Rating was 123. His Speed Figure for this race – worked out by an arcane formula taking into account such factors as weight, going, wind and the distance between horses – was 94.

Faithful Son, second here, had also run in race 2011: indeed, he had won it (indicated by the asterisk). His official rating going into this race was 115. He was beaten half a length by Daylami, and started 5–1 third favourite. The betting percentages added up to 115.6 per cent, making the book 15.6 per cent over-round (see page 58). Seven horses ran in the race.

Below the list of runners is yet more information. The time of the winner of the Eclipse was 2 minutes 6.82 seconds, 0.12 seconds above (i.e. slower than) Raceform Standard Time.

The Computer Straight Forecast (see page 67) paid £8.80. Tote returns (see page 68) were £2.60 for the win on Daylami (that is, 1.6–1, slightly better than the starting price of 6–4), £1.60 for the place on Daylami and £3.10 for the place on Faithful Son; dual forecast Daylami and Faithful Son to finish first and second in either order paid £4.80.

## 2550 CORAL-ECLIPSE STKS (Gp 1) (3-Y.O+) (Class A)
4-05 (4-06) **1m 2f 7y** £147,600.00 (£55,100.00: £26,350.00: £11,350.00) Stalls: High GOING minus 0.14 sec per fur (G)

| | | | SP | RR | SF |
|---|---|---|---|---|---|
| 2011[3] **Daylami (IRE)** (SbinSuroor) **4-9-7** LDettori(5) (chsd ldr over 1f: chsd ldr over 2f out: led over 1f out: hrd rdn: r.o wl) | — | 1 | 6/4[1] | 123 | 94 |
| 2011* **Faithful Son (USA)** (115) (SbinSuroor) **4-9-7** JReid(1) (lw: stdy hdwy 2f out: chsd wnr fnl f: hrd rdn: r.o) | ½ | 2 | 5/1[3] | 122 | 93 |
| 2105[4] **Central Park (IRE)** (118) (SbinSuroor) **3-8-10** DO'Donohoe(7) (lw: led over 8f: wknd ins fnl f) | 6 | 3 | 14/1 | 113 | 73 |
| 2011[7] **Insatiable (IRE)** (120) (SirMichaelStoute) **5-9-7** MJKinane(2) (plld hrd: hmpd on ins 2f out: swtchd lft wl over 1f out: nvr nr to chal) | ½ | 4 | 100/30[2] | 112 | 83 |
| 2010[3] **Poteen (USA)** (119) (LMCumani) **4-9-7** WRSwinbum(6) (lw: a.p: hrd rdn over 1f out: wknd fnl f) | ¾ | 5 | 9/1 | 111 | 82 |
| 2011[6] **Taipan (IRE)** (120) (JLDunlop) **6-9-7** PatEddery(4) (chsd ldr over 8f out tl over 2f out: sn wknd) | ½ | 6 | 14/1 | 110 | 81 |
| 2012[3] **Duck Row (USA)** (112) (JARToller) **3-8-10** SSanders(3) (lw: rdn & hdwy 3f out: wknd over 1f out) | 3½ | 7 | 7/1 | 104 | 64 |

(SP 115.6%) **7 Rn**

**2m 6.82** (0.12) CSF £8.80 TOTE £2.60: £1.60 £3.10 (£4.80) OWNER Godolphin (NEWMARKET) BRED Aga Khan's Studs
WEIGHT FOR AGE 3yo-11lb

**IN-FOCUS: It has to be said that this was a slightly sub-standard Eclispe, but it saw Frankie Dettori lift the race for the first time and the Godolphin team saddled the first three home - a Group 1 first in this country and a feat that will surely never be surpassed.**

**2011 Daylami (IRE)** gained revenge over Faithful Son for his unlucky defeat in the Prince of Wales's Stakes. Looming up large a quarter of a mile from home, he gained a definite advantage below the distance and, responding to pressure, just kept his old adversary at bay. Connections believe he will stay a mile and a half and he will now head for the King George VI and Queen Elizabeth Diamond Stakes. (6/4)

**2011* Faithful Son (USA)** was unable to confirm Prince of Wales's form with the winner on 5lb worse terms. Nevertheless, he made sure the winner did not have things all his own way and, sticking to his guns commendably, finished well clear of the remainder. Another Group race should soon come his way. (5/1: 3/1-11/2)

**2105 Central Park (IRE)** attempted to make all the running. Eventually collared below the distance, he was left standing by the front two in the final furlong. Nevertheless, this was still a good effort. (14/1)

**2011 Insatiable (IRE)** again failed to reproduce his Brigadier Gerard form. Admittedly he was done no favours along the inside rail a quarter of a mile from home, which cost him ground he could ill afford. He did stay on in the closing stages, but never threatened to get near the principals. (100/30)

**2010 Poteen (USA)** may well have found this longer trip a bit too much for, coming under pressure below the distance, he ran out of puff up the hill. (9/1)

**2011 Taipan (IRE)** may have won two extremely valuable Group One events abroad last year, but these rivals proved too hot for him and, collared for second place over two furlongs from home, soon had bellows to mend. (14/1)

**2012 Duck Row (USA)** quite simply failed to stay the trip, for having moved up on the outside early in the straight he had run out of steam below the distance. (7/1)

Daylami is owned by Godolphin, trained at Newmarket, bred by the Aga Khan's Studs.

By the Weight-for-Age scale, three-year-olds carried eleven pounds less than their elders.

The 'In-Focus' comment draws attention to a particular feature of the race, and the note-book comments analyse the performance in more depth than the bare bones of the in-running description, pointing the way towards future possibilities (for example, Poteen might benefit from a shorter trip). This section also marks any notable market moves: Faithful Son, for example, started at 5–1 but moved in the market between 3–1 and 11–2.

*Opposite:* The card in the *Racing Post* for the Samsung Electronics Scottish Champion Hurdle at Ayr on 18 April 1998.

This is a Grade 2, Class A event over two miles, due off at 3.25, and to be shown live on Channel Four; first prize £15,699.99. There are four declared runners.

The race conditions indicate that £25,000 has been added to the owners' entry money; that the race is for four-year-olds and older, and the highest weight to be carried is eleven stone eleven pounds; that the weights have been raised fourteen pounds, the difference in the original handicap between today's top weight Large Action and the original top weight, who is not running; that no horse may carry a weight of less than ten stone four pounds; that there are no penalties for the race once the weights have been published; that the official handicap mark of the top weight Large Action is 148; that there were originally thirteen entries; and that the prize money is as listed.

Large Action will carry number 1. He was foaled in Ireland ('IRE'), it is seventy-seven days since his last outing, and he has won over this distance ('C' would indicate that he had won at this course, and 'CD' that he had won at this distance at this course); he is a bay gelding by The Parson out of Ballayadam Lass; he is a ten-year-old carrying eleven stone seven pounds; he is trained by O. Sherwood and owned by B. T. Stewart-Brown, and is to be ridden by J. A. McCarthy. His rating for this race in the *Racing Post*'s own handicap Postmark is 160. The abbreviated form line immediately to the left of Large Action's name shows that he was fourth on his last run, pulled up ('P') the time before that, sixth the time before that. Form before the dash ('1PP') indicates his last three runs the previous season. (Other letters found in the form line indicate as follows: 'F' means fell; 'U' means unseated rider; 'B' means brought down; 'R' means refused.)

Blowing Wind was foaled in France, is a bay or brown gelding, and the printing of his Postmark in a black circle indicates that he is considered best in of the four runners at these weights. Padre Mio has had three previous runs this season, but did not run at all last season: the oblique in his form line indicates that the first three runs ('666') were in the season before last.

Then follow brief details of the 1997 running of this race (winner Shadow Leader was evens favourite and ran off an official mark of 136), the betting forecast and runner-by-runner analysis before a summing-up and selections from two of the paper's other form columns, Postdata and Top Speed.

Not much doubt about which horse to be on here – and Blowing Wind duly obliged at 6–5 on.

## 3.25 Samsung Electronics Scottish Champion Hurdle (Class A) (Grade 2)

**CH4**

4 declared

Winner £15,669.99

2m

£25,000 added **For** 4yo+ **Weights** Highest weight 11st 7lb **Weights raised 14lb Minimum Weight** 10-4 **Penalties** (no penalties after publication of weights) **Large Action's Handicap Mark 148 Entries 13 pay £125 Penalty Value 1st £15,669.99 2nd £5,929.75 3rd £2,902.38 4th £1,322.88**

| | | | |
|---|---|---|---|
| 1PP-6P4 | **LARGE ACTION** (IRE) 77 D | | 10 11-7 |
| **1** | b g The Parson–Ballyadam Lass | | J A McCarthy (160) |
| | O Sherwood B T Stewart-Brown | | |
| 2361253 | **KERAWI** 14 D | | 5 11-6 |
| **2** | b g Warning–Kerali | | C Llewellyn (161) |
| | N A Twiston-Davies Matt Archer & Miss Jean Broadhurst | | |
| 7248311 | **BLOWING WIND** (FR) 30 D | | 5 11-5 |
| **3** | b/br g Fabulous Dancer–Bassita | | R Dunwoody (162) |
| | M C Pipe P A Deal | | |
| 666/246 | **PADRE MIO** (IRE) 140 D | | 10 10-5 |
| **4** | b g The Parson–Mwanamio | | G Bradley (153) |
| | C P E Brooks Lady Lloyd Webber | | |

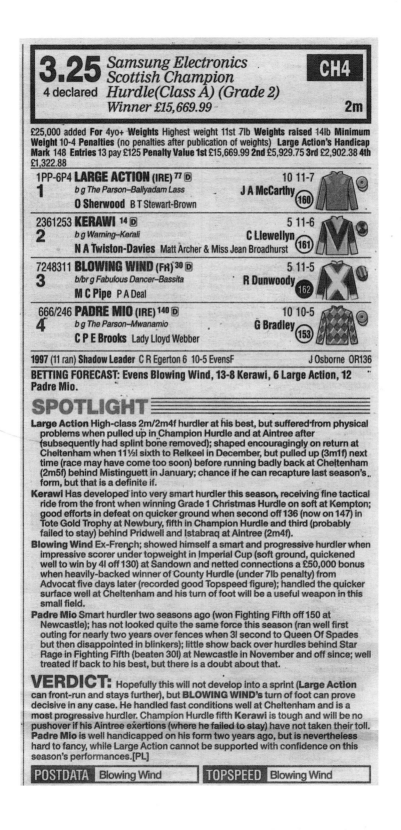

**1997** (11 ran) Shadow Leader C R Egerton 6 10-5 EvensF J Osborne OR136

**BETTING FORECAST: Evens Blowing Wind, 13-8 Kerawi, 6 Large Action, 12 Padre Mio.**

## SPOTLIGHT

**Large Action** High-class 2m/2m4f hurdler at his best, but suffered from physical problems when pulled up in Champion Hurdle and at Aintree after (subsequently had splint bone removed); shaped encouragingly on return at Cheltenham when 11½l sixth to Relkeel in December, but pulled up (3m1f) next time (race may have come too soon) before running badly back at Cheltenham (2m5f) behind Mistinguett in January; chance if he can recapture last season's form, but that is a definite if.

**Kerawi** Has developed into very smart hurdler this season, receiving fine tactical ride from the front when winning Grade 1 Christmas Hurdle on soft at Kempton; good efforts in defeat on quicker ground when second off 136 (now on 147) in Tote Gold Trophy at Newbury, fifth in Champion Hurdle and third (probably failed to stay) behind Pridwell and Istabraq at Aintree (2m4f).

**Blowing Wind** Ex-French; showed himself a smart and progressive hurdler when impressive scorer under topweight in Imperial Cup (soft ground, quickened well to win by 4l off 130) at Sandown and netted connections a £50,000 bonus when heavily-backed winner of County Hurdle (under 7lb penalty) from Advocat five days later (recorded good Topspeed figure); handled the quicker surface well at Cheltenham and his turn of foot will be a useful weapon in this small field.

**Padre Mio** Smart hurdler two seasons ago (won Fighting Fifth off 150 at Newcastle); has not looked quite the same force this season (ran well first outing for nearly two years over fences when 3l second to Queen Of Spades but then disappointed in blinkers); little show back over hurdles behind Star Rage in Fighting Fifth (beaten 30l) at Newcastle in November and off since; well treated if back to his best, but there is a doubt about that.

## VERDICT:
Hopefully this will not develop into a sprint (**Large Action** can front-run and stays further), but **BLOWING WIND's** turn of foot can prove decisive in any case. He handled fast conditions well at Cheltenham and is a most progressive hurdler. Champion Hurdle fifth **Kerawi** is tough and will be no pushover if his Aintree exertions (where he failed to stay) have not taken their toll. **Padre Mio** is well handicapped on his form two years ago, but is nevertheless hard to fancy, while Large Action cannot be supported with confidence on this season's performances.[PL]

| POSTDATA | Blowing Wind | TOPSPEED | Blowing Wind |
|---|---|---|---|

The on-course jungle. *Above:* Rails bookmakers at Cheltenham; *below:* Shouting the odds at Sandown Park; *opposite, above:* Tic-tac Mickey 'Hokey' Stuart in full flight; *opposite, below:* Making a book.

Alternatives to the on-course jungle. *Above:* Calm before the storm
at Tote windows at Cheltenham; *below:* Quiet contemplation of
the action in an Esher betting shop.

The two biggest races of the betting year: *Above:* Over Becher's Brook in the 1981 Grand National won by Aldaniti; *below:* The storming finish of the 1998 Derby, with High-Rise (Olivier Peslier) getting up to head City Honours (John Reid).

Three big losers . . . *Above:* Greville Starkey and Dancing Brave fail to collar
Walter Swinburn and Shahrastani in the 1986 Derby; *below:* The Fellow
*(extreme left)* labours up the Cheltenham hill as winner Jodami *(hooped sleeves)*
and Rushing Wild take the last in the 1993 Gold Cup; *opposite, above:* Gaelic Storm
is lost in the pack as Superior Premium storms home to land the 1998 Stewards' Cup.

. . . and one big winner: Nashwan (Willie Carson, striped cap)
powers up the Newmarket straight to land the 1989 Two Thousand Guineas.

# Betting –
# and how to do it

# Big Mac's guide
# to the betting jungle
## John McCririck

So Jimbo has put you straight on all the mysteries of form and what to do with it. You've studied the race, scrutinised the runners in the paddock, and made your selection. Now it's time to put your money where your mouth is – and bet!

Come into the steaming jungle of the betting ring, that bubbling cauldron of activity where every day hundreds of thousands of pounds are won and lost. Here's where you are buffeted by punters desperate to get the 'ear 'ole' (6–4) while it lasts, where you pick up, or 'earwig', last-minute gossip and rumours, where wads of money go into – and sometimes out of – bookies' satchels.

It's noisy, it's frenetic, it can be manic – and there's nowhere like it on earth.

Not everybody is able to join in the cut and thrust of the racecourse ring: 95 per cent of wagering on horses in Britain takes place in betting shops or on credit, and some of you have the luxury of striking your bet over the phone as you watch Channel Four Racing – though turn the sound down when that burbling, arm-waving fatso in the betting ring comes on!

However you bet, contemplate my golden rules – without, please, pausing to wonder whether I've always kept to them myself. If I have, why am I, a failed 'investor' and bookmaker, still scratching a meagre living with Channel Four? . . .

- *Bet within your means* The most obvious advice, but one which some people sadly ignore: never, *ever*, bet more than you can afford to lose. Decide in advance your limit, and don't exceed it – however tempting that bet in the desperate Getting Out Stakes. Always remember there's another day. It's a perfectly natural desire to be 'in front' and leave course or betting shop with that glow of satisfaction – and bulging pockets – but never chase your losses. So simple to write!

- *Be disciplined* Unlike bookmakers, you don't have to bet on every race. The exercise of patience, waiting for the right betting opportunity, is a vital weapon in any good punter's artillery, and all the professional punters – yes, there are some who really do make a living from the game – are celebrated for their patience. Exercise restraint, and you'll do much better in the long term.

- *Come racing!* Never mind lying in your pit at home watching those know-alls on Channel Four. Come racing, where there are crucial betting advantages which I've listed on pages 85–6.

- *Keep records* Systematic recording of all your bets reveals patterns and preferences from which you can benefit, and the effort of disciplined record-keeping will be well rewarded. At the very least record:
  - date
  - stake
  - type of bet – and whether placed well in advance of race or just before
  - selection(s)
  - odds – and whether this was a board price, SP, ante-post, etc.
  - type of race
  - result
  - running balance of year's betting (which can be very instructive!) Jimbo McGrath has revealed that he has staked around £6 million in a lifetime on the Turf and is more than £600,000 (tax free!) in front. Each wager is recorded. You wouldn't want to be Jimbo's bookie!

Periodically study your records for valuable insights into your punting strengths and weaknesses. What you discover will be potentially profitable in the future. It could be to avoid handicaps, or betting odds-on. Sometimes the trends revealed can be alarming. Learn from them.

- *Shop around* Never rush in to take the first price you see. In the morning, weigh up the range of prices published in the press. On course, take a look at all prices available in the ring. Work out the value price you reckon your fancy should be offered at. Resolve never to take less. With sound judgement of odds the winners missed will be more than made up for by avoiding taking a chance with those underpriced.

- *Study the statistics* When that moron on Channel Four Racing starts banging on about 'only four winning favourites in thirty-one runnings of this race', don't switch over. The statistical profile of some races can be extremely significant, and it's yet another factor to bear in mind when making a bet. Of the last thirty-six runnings of the Derby, twenty-four – two-thirds – have gone to the first or second favourite. Only three favourites have won the Scottish National since the war, and of the last forty-two runnings of the Ayr Gold Cup, just three have been won by the favourite. In which race would you be more comfortable backing a market leader?

- *Back to basics!* Punters who do not understand the basic principles of betting are putting themselves at a hopeless disadvantage in the perpetual battle against the bookies. You don't need a master's degree in maths – I couldn't even pass my Elementary Maths O-Level – but get a grasp of the bare essentials and in the long run your betting will be much more efficient – and profitable.

Stick to those few gems of good sense and you'll be well equipped to hold your own in the tantalising, exhilarating but so often frustrating world of wagering.

Good luck!

# Betting basics

A punter wanting to bet on a horse has a choice:

- to bet with a bookmaker, who prices up the race on the basis of his assessment of the chances of each horse and then alters those odds according to the flow of money on each particular runner; or
- to bet with the Tote, a pool system where the backers all put their money in and the winners share the payout.
- to bet 'on the spread', where you can buy or sell on your opinion whether the firm's view of an outcome is too high or too low (see page 78).

Bookmakers' odds lengthen (offering a higher return) or shorten (offering a lower one) according to how money is being wagered, but the odds at which you strike your bet remain valid for that transaction whatever happens subsequently, unless you bet at starting price – the odds at which the horse is officially declared to have started the race.

On the Tote, you will not know the exact return on your stake until after the race.

Spread betting can involve huge gains, or losses, though back-up positions can usually be taken as the bet unfolds.

## Odds

Odds are simply an expression of probability: a way of representing the likelihood, as perceived by the person laying the odds, of the horse winning or losing. (We'll come on to each-way betting later.)

So, a bookie who quotes a particular horse at evens (1–1) thinks that there is an equal (50 per cent) chance of the horse winning and losing. At 2–1 against there is a 33.33 per cent chance of its winning and a 66.67 per cent chance of its losing: that is, two out of every three chances – 2 plus 1 equals 3 – are against its winning. At 2–1 on (the 'on' indicating that the odds are reversed, '2–1 on' being the common way of expressing 1–2) there is a 66.67 per cent chance of its winning and a 33.33 per cent chance of its losing. So any horse at 'odds on' is deemed more likely to win than lose. (A useful way of thinking about odds is that, with odds against, the first number expressed is the multiple of your stake that you will win, the second number the amount that the bookie will keep if you lose – or, if you like, your stake unit. Thus at 6–1 against you put down one to win six.)

Note that these are judgements of the perceived likelihood of a particular outcome – perceived, that is, by the bookmaker. The canny way to approach betting is to weigh up your own opinion of the horse's chance of winning against the bookmaker's, and to back your fancy if the odds on offer are longer than you feel represent that chance: such a bet represents 'value', the 'bargain' which every regular punter seeks.

**Big Mac says . . .**

*Judge all the factors involved. Then assess, objectively, the likely probability of any horse winning. If the odds on offer are far bigger, check for any late developments – sweating or unruly behaviour in the paddock, going down to post badly or negatives in the betting ring. If you still believe the price is tempting, step in. If not, keep out!*

## Odds

Occasionally people are perplexed by what commonly expressed odds – 6–5, say, or 13–8 – actually mean. This list gives a few of the odds frequently quoted in horse racing expressed in more familiar fractions:

| | | | |
|---|---|---|---|
| Evens | 1 to 1 | 9–4 | $2\frac{1}{4}$ to 1 |
| 11–10 | $1\frac{1}{10}$ to 1 | 5–2 | $2\frac{1}{2}$ to 1 |
| 6–5 | $1\frac{1}{5}$ to 1 | 11–4 | $2\frac{3}{4}$ to 1 |
| 5–4 | $1\frac{1}{4}$ to 1 | 100–30 | $3\frac{1}{3}$ to 1 |
| 11–8 | $1\frac{3}{8}$ to 1 | 7–2 | $3\frac{1}{2}$ to 1 |
| 6–4 | $1\frac{1}{2}$ to 1 | 9–2 | $4\frac{1}{2}$ to 1 |
| 13–8 | $1\frac{5}{8}$ to 1 | 11–2 | $5\frac{1}{2}$ to 1 |
| 7–4 | $1\frac{3}{4}$ to 1 | 13–2 | $6\frac{1}{2}$ to 1 |
| 15–8 | $1\frac{7}{8}$ to 1 | 15–2 | $7\frac{1}{2}$ to 1 |
| 85–40 | $2\frac{1}{8}$ to 1 | 17–2 | $8\frac{1}{2}$ to 1 |

## Odds percentages

| Odds on | Price | Odds against | Odds on | Price | Odds against |
|---|---|---|---|---|---|
| 50.00 | Evens | 50.00 | 87.50 | 7–1 | 12.50 |
| 52.38 | 11–10 | 47.62 | 88.24 | 15–2 | 11.76 |
| 54.55 | 6–5 | 45.45 | 88.89 | 8–1 | 11.11 |
| 55.56 | 5–4 | 44.44 | 89.47 | 17–2 | 10.53 |
| 57.89 | 11–8 | 42.11 | 90.00 | 9–1 | 10.00 |
| 60.00 | 6–4 | 40.00 | 90.91 | 10–1 | 9.09 |
| 61.90 | 13–8 | 38.10 | 91.67 | 11–1 | 8.33 |
| 63.64 | 7–4 | 36.36 | 92.31 | 12–1 | 7.69 |
| 65.22 | 15–8 | 34.78 | 92.86 | 13–1 | 7.14 |
| 66.67 | 2–1 | 33.33 | 93.33 | 14–1 | 6.67 |
| 68.00 | 85–40 | 32.00 | 93.75 | 15–1 | 6.25 |
| 69.23 | 9–4 | 30.77 | 94.12 | 16–1 | 5.88 |
| 71.43 | 5–2 | 28.57 | 95.24 | 20–1 | 4.76 |
| 73.33 | 11–4 | 26.67 | 95.65 | 22–1 | 4.35 |
| 75.00 | 3–1 | 25.00 | 96.15 | 25–1 | 3.85 |
| 76.92 | 100–30 | 23.08 | 97.06 | 33–1 | 2.94 |
| 77.78 | 7–2 | 22.22 | 97.56 | 40–1 | 2.44 |
| 80.00 | 4–1 | 20.00 | 98.04 | 50–1 | 1.96 |
| 81.82 | 9–2 | 18.18 | 98.51 | 66–1 | 1.49 |
| 83.33 | 5–1 | 16.67 | 98.77 | 80–1 | 1.23 |
| 84.62 | 11–2 | 15.38 | 99.01 | 100–1 | 0.99 |
| 85.71 | 6–1 | 14.29 | 99.60 | 250–1 | 0.40 |
| 86.67 | 13–2 | 13.33 | 99.80 | 500–1 | 0.20 |

## Betting with a bookmaker

A lot of people find the mysteries of betting with a bookmaker – the maths, the jargon, the ritual, to say nothing of the associated arm-waving of men in white gloves – completely impenetrable. And yet the majority of the population have a bet with a bookie at least once a year, even if it is just £1 each way on the Grand National, on which some £80 million was supposedly staked in 1998.

In fact, the principle of betting with a bookmaker is simple: he offers odds at which you may pitch your money against his. The practice and the maths, however, can be less clear. Nor is confusion restricted to the arcane refinements of multiple wagers: one of the most widespread mistakes about betting is that once you've handed your stake over to the bookie that's the last you see of it – even if your horse wins and you get a handsome return. But if that were the case, why would anyone ever bet at odds on?

If your betting is to be effective, you need to know not only how to do it yourself, but how the betting market works, and that means understanding the mathematical factors that govern it. You may think this doesn't matter; but the bookmakers don't, and unless you know the rudiments of how a book is constructed you'll be putting yourself at a disadvantage to start with. Conversely, a punter who knows how a book works and what factors affect the prices is a punter well poised to take advantage of market moves.

### The over-round book

Face facts. The average punter cannot win, for it is the bookmaker who constructs the odds (the 'book') for each race – and he does so in such a way that, in the long term, he will make a profit. How?

Mathematically, if the probabilities of winning of all the horses in a particular race are added up, they must total exactly 100 per cent. What the bookmaker does to guarantee his profitability is ensure that the total of the percentage probabilities he quotes – the odds he offers – for each race exceeds 100 per cent.

As an example, we can look at the returned starting prices for the 1998 Vodafone Derby:

| Horse | SP | % |
|---|---|---|
| Cape Verdi | 11–4 | 26.67 |
| Second Empire | 9–2 | 18.18 |
| Greek Dance | 5–1 | 16.67 |
| King Of Kings | 11–2 | 15.38 |
| City Honours | 12–1 | 7.69 |
| Gulland | 12–1 | 7.69 |
| Courteous | 14–1 | 6.67 |
| Haami | 20–1 | 4.76 |
| High-Rise | 20–1 | 4.76 |
| Saratoga Springs | 20–1 | 4.76 |
| The Glow-Worm | 20–1 | 4.76 |
| Border Arrow | 25–1 | 3.85 |
| Sadian | 25–1 | 3.85 |
| Mutamam | 50–1 | 1.96 |
| Sunshine Street | 150–1 | 0.66 |
| total percentages | | 128.31 |

In strictly mathematical terms, the total of those percentages should be 100 – yet the actual total is over 128. That difference represents the layers' theoretical profit.

A book in which the probabilies add up to over 100 per cent is described as 'over-round', and in this case the book is over-round by 28.31 per cent, which means that for every £128.31 the bookmaker takes in bets, he theoretically expects to have to pay out £100, leaving him £28.31 profit. When a book is over-round the punter cannot back every runner and be guaranteed a return, and as every efficient bookmaker will be betting over-round this quickly disposes of the notion that you can win by backing every horse in a race.

Bookmakers do not, of course, take money evenly across the whole field, nor do they win on every race; but by maintaining the over-roundness of the book they are ensuring that in the long term they will have to pay out less than they take in. (A set of odds in which the aggregate percentages total under 100 is described as 'overbroke'.)

### Comparing the odds

Comparing the odds offered by different bookmakers is the key to finding the best value in a race. Every day the *Racing Post* publishes the Pricewise column with a chart comparing the early prices on that day's major events, as well as regular ante-post updates. Very occasionally these will indicate ways in which, by shopping around and backing different runners with different bookmakers – usually in small fields – you can find an 'overbroke' book and guarantee yourself a win.

Several national newspapers now provide a similar service.

### Constructing the book

For the really big races the betting will begin a long way in advance of the event – weeks, even months, occasionally years in advance. For other key races the major bookmakers advertise prices on the morning of the race, and punters may back at these prices – which may go up and down according to the amounts of money being wagered – until the proper book is formed before the race itself. (A 'steamer' is a horse which has been heavily backed off-course before the actual pre-race market has been formed.)

---

Books tend to be more over-round in competitive handicaps: the book for the John Smith's Cup at York in 1998, won by Porto Foricos, was over-round by 45.2 per cent.

---

The bookmakers employ form and betting experts to draw up the 'tissue', a forecast of how the betting on the race will open on the course, and the course bookmakers (whose activities dictate the officially returned starting price) will probably start out betting to these prices, adjusting them subsequently according to the general response to these prices and to their own judgement of the probable outcome of the race. The more punters back the winner, and the longer the odds at which they do so, the more the bookie is going to have to pay out; so if he takes a lot of money on one horse he will shorten its price in order to dissuade other punters from backing it, while if (for whatever reason) he thinks that a horse will not win, or he can't lay it, he will lengthen its price in order to tempt punters who think they know better than he does.

While all this is going on – bets being made, prices adjusted, judgements formed – the bookmaker will be constantly aware of his own liabilities, and if what he stands to have to pay out on one horse is more than he can comfortably cover from losing bets on the other runners he may decide to 'lay off' – that is, to pass all or some of the money he has taken on that horse on to other bookmakers – in other words, betting on that horse himself. It is these transactions, the bets made by course bookies among themselves, that are communicated by the sign language of 'tic tac'.

---

Uniquely, on Channel Four each betting show is accompanied by the current betting percentage so, at a glance, the updated figure in favour of the bookies is clear.

---

The biggest movements of money, however, are not between the course bookies, but between the off-course bookmakers and their counterparts at the track: for all the money wagered away from the course, in betting shops and through credit accounts with the big bookmakers, has to be brought into the ring in order that the returned starting prices – which are determined by the on-course market – accurately reflect the weight of money wagered on the race. This is done through representatives of the off-course bookmakers, some of whom will bet at the track to put their off-course money into the market, others sending bets through by means of the 'blower', a telephone service which relays money to the course bookmakers. The 'magic sign' is the tic-tac signal (somewhat like drawing a halo over the head) which indicates money from Ladbrokes – the largest bookmaker in Britain – being brought into the market.

## Types of bet

There are many different types of bet, some of them involving procedures and permutations of brain-aching complexity. Combination bets, despite the demands they make on the mental powers of the backer, and despite the fact that they are difficult to pull off, are attractive to small punters as they offer the promise of big returns for modest outlay.

The most usual types of bet, and some of the more exotic, are described briefly here, with sample calculations which exclude any allowance for tax (see page 75).

### Win

You bet on the horse to come first. The tax-free return on a £5 win bet at 6–1 is £35: £5 stake plus £30 winnings. In a betting shop, with the customary 9 per cent deduction, it is £31.85.

### Each way

You bet on the horse either to win or to be placed – that is, to finish in the first two in races of five, six or seven runners, the first three in races of eight or more runners, or the first four in handicaps with sixteen or more runners. These stipulations can alter from one bookmaker to another, and some pay out on the fifth place in very competitive big races. Shop around for the best terms.

The odds for a place are normally one-quarter or one-fifth the odds for a win, depending on the nature of the race and the number of runners: the bookmaker will advertise the fraction.

An each-way bet is in fact two bets – one for the win and one for the place – and consequently the stake will be twice the unit of the bet: thus a bet of £5 each way costs £10. A bet of £5 each way (with the place odds one-quarter the win odds) on a horse which wins at 10–1 returns winnings of £62.50 (£50 win plus £12.50 place, as the winning horse is also placed) plus your stake of £10 – a total return (tax-free) of £72.50. If the horse is second you win £12.50 and have your stake on the place bet returned, but lose your £5 win bet: so your return on the £10 invested is £17.50. Obviously it is not worth backing a horse each way if its odds are much less than 5–1, as the amount you will make on the place bet if it is placed but does not win will not cover your loss on the win bet: the calculations for off-course bets are further complicated by the need to allow for tax, but it should be clear that an on-course each-way bet at 4–1, one-quarter the odds a place, will yield no gain and no loss if the horse is placed but does not win.

## Place

Not many bookmakers will bet for place only, though the Tote runs a Place pool on every race with five or more runners (see page 70).

## Combination bets

These are individual bets which combine two or more horses in a single wager: if one horse loses the whole bet is lost. The permutations are infinite, but the most common versions include the following.

*Double* You bet on two horses in different races. If the first wins, the return – winnings and stake – go on to the second.

A simple way of calculating the winnings on a double is to add one to each of the odds, multiply them, subtract one from the total and multiply by the stake. A £5 double on horses which both win at 2–1 is an 8–1 double, yielding a return of £45 – £40 winnings plus £5 stake – as the first win gives a return of £15, which then goes on the second horse at 2–1 and brings £30 winnings plus £15 stake: £45.

You will not get a bookmaker to accept a double bet calculated in this way on two events where the first result has a direct bearing on the second. For instance, had you wanted to back King Of Kings to win the Two Thousand Guineas and the Derby in 1998, the odds quoted would have been shorter than a simple multiple of the single odds for both eventualities, as success in the first would significantly increase the chances of success in the second.

*Treble* You bet on three horses in different races. Again, add one to each of the winning odds, multiply them, and subtract one from the total to find the winnings. So a £5 treble on three horses which each win at 2–1 yields a return of £135: winnings of £130 plus the £5 stake.

*Accumulator* On the same principle, you bet on any number of horses to win different races, calculating the winnings in the same way as for a double or a treble. The old ITV Seven was a seven-horse accumulator: had your seven choices in a £5 accumulator all obliged at 2–1 you would have relieved your bookmaker of £10,930 in winnings.

### Multiple bets

These are ways of combining different bets on several horses in various ways. Unlike combination bets, success does not depend on each horse winning: the names under which such bets go are simply a shorthand for a recognized menu of individual bets. Multiple bets can be win or each way.

*Patent* Combines three different horses in different races in seven separate bets – three singles, three doubles, and one treble.
    Thus if the three horses selected are Angelic, Buttercup and Cowpat, the Patent consists of:

| | |
|---|---|
| 3 singles on | Angelic |
| | Buttercup |
| | Cowpat |
| 3 doubles: | Angelic with Buttercup |
| | Angelic with Cowpat |
| | Buttercup with Cowpat |
| 1 treble: | Angelic with Buttercup with Cowpat |

A £1 win Patent will cost you £7; a £1 each-way Patent costs £14. Say you have a £1 win Patent on Angelic, Buttercup and Cowpat and they all win at 2–1; your winnings are:

£6 (three £1 singles each winning at 2–1); plus
£24 (three £1 doubles with each horse winning at 2–1); plus
£26 (a £1 treble with each horse winning at 2–1), producing a
    total of £56.

If two of the horses win at 2–1 while the third loses, you would still make a profit. You win £4 (two £1 singles each winning at 2–1) plus £8 (one £1 double with each horse winning at 2–1: total winnings £12. But of your seven bets four (one single, two doubles, one treble) have lost, so your profit is £12 less £4: £8.

A Patent without the singles is a *Trixie* – three horses combined in three doubles and one treble (four bets).

*Yankee* Combines four different horses in different races in eleven bets (so a £1 win Yankee costs £11). The horses are connected in

- six doubles
- four trebles
- one four-horse accumulator.

(A Lucky 15 is a fifteen-bet wager adding four singles to the eleven bets of the Yankee. If one selection wins but the other four lose, many bookmakers will benevolently double the odds for your single winning bet.)

Have a Yankee on the three horses we've just backed in a Patent and a fourth, Dunderhead. The bet looks like this:

| 6 doubles | Angelic and Buttercup |
|-----------|----------------------|
|           | Angelic and Cowpat |
|           | Angelic and Dunderhead |
|           | Buttercup and Cowpat |
|           | Buttercup and Dunderhead |
|           | Cowpat and Dunderhead |

| 4 trebles | Angelic, Buttercup, Cowpat |
|-----------|----------------------------|
|           | Angelic, Cowpat, Dunderhead |
|           | Angelic, Buttercup, Dunderhead |
|           | Buttercup, Cowpat, Dunderhead |

| 1 accumulator | Angelic, Buttercup, Cowpat, Dunderhead |
|---------------|----------------------------------------|

Should all four win at 2–1, our £1 win Yankee wins . . . no, work it out for yourself!

*Super Yankee* Combines five selections in

- ten doubles
- ten trebles
- five four-horse accumulators
- one five-horse accumulator

– a total of twenty-six bets. (A Super Yankee is also known as a Canadian.)

*Heinz* Combines six selections in fifty-seven bets:

- fifteen doubles
- twenty trebles
- fifteen four-horse accumulators
- six five-horse accumulators
- one six-horse accumulator.

*Super Heinz* Combines seven selections in 120 bets:

- twenty-one doubles
- thirty-five trebles
- thirty-five four-horse accumulators
- twenty-one five-horse accumulators
- seven six-horse accumulators
- one seven-horse accumulator.

*Goliath* Combines eight selections in 247 bets:

- twenty-eight doubles
- fifty-six trebles
- seventy four-horse accumulators
- fifty-six five-horse accumulators
- twenty-eight six-horse accumulators
- eight seven-horse accumulators
- one eight-horse accumulator.

## Speciality bets

These apply to just one race and include:

*Forecast* The Tote Dual Forecast involves giving the first and second horses in either order.

The Computer Straight Forecast is a betting-shop wager which involves predicting the first two in correct order (so called because the dividend is calculated by computer, using a formula too complex for mortal man to comprehend).

*Tricast* In handicaps of eight or more declared runners and no fewer than six actual runners, the punter must select the first three in correct order. Again, a computer calculates the dividend.

---

Heard that some horse is a racing certainty? Consider this . . .
At Chepstow on 28 June 1947 Glendower, ridden by Gordon Richards, started at 20–1 on to beat his solitary opponent, Markwell. This was in the days before starting stalls, and as the tapes of the old-style starting gate went up Glendower whipped round and unseated the great jockey, leaving Markwell to win unopposed. Gordon Richards related this embarrassing tale in his autobiography, adding: 'I heard afterwards that a certain gentleman was in the habit of picking out my best ride of the day, and then ringing up his bookmaker and backing it to win one thousand pounds. On that day he selected Glendower, but he did not anticipate that I would start at twenty to one on. That race cost him twenty thousand pounds.'
A salutary lesson for those ready to stake twenty grand. Yet Glendower was not the shortest-priced loser that Gordon Richards ever rode. In the Clarence House Stakes at Ascot on 23 September 1948 he partnered Royal Forest, who started at 25–1 on to beat three opponents (all 33–1 against) – one of whom, Burpham, beat the favourite half a length.

---

## The Tote

Betting with the Tote – the Horserace Totalisator Board – is based on a simple principle. All the money bet on all the horses in a race goes into a pot or 'pool'; following the race, this pool is shared out among all those who have placed winning bets.

The picture is complicated slightly by the deductions that are made from the pool before payout to cover running costs, including contributions to racecourses and to the Betting Levy.

There are separate pools for the different sorts of bet, and each pool is subjected to a different level of deduction: in 1998 the deductions were:

- 16 per cent from the Win pool
- 24 per cent from the Place pool
- 29 per cent each from the Dual Forecast, Jackpot and Trifecta
- 27 per cent from the Placepot
- 26 per cent from the Quadpot

A simple example will show how this works. Say the Win pool for a race consists of £10,000, of which one thousand £1 bets have been staked on the horse which wins:

| | |
|---|---|
| pool | £10,000 |
| deduction | £1,600 |
| payout | £8,400 |
| dividend | £8.40 per £1 ticket |

The dividend (or 'Tote return') is declared to a £1 unit and includes the stake, so the actual winnings in the above example are £7.40. All the other pools operate in the same way as the Win pool.

The Tote screens at racecourses will show you approximate Tote odds as the betting takes place before a race, but you cannot know exactly what the dividend will be until after the race, and this is the crucial difference between betting with the Tote and with a bookmaker: with a bookmaker you bet either at starting price or at the price which he quotes you or has displayed, and your bet remains at that price regardless of how many other people place bets after you, and at what odds; with the Tote you will not know when you make the bet precisely what the return will be, as it will be affected by all the people who place their bets after you. Off-course you have even less chance of seeing the likely return: it is not possible for the television viewer to know how the Tote odds are looking just before the race, and some off-course betting shops do not bet at Tote odds.

Because Tote and bookies operate on different principles, their odds usually differ; but neither side is consistently favoured by the discrepancy.

The Tote is a big player in British racing and a prominent presence as a race sponsor – notably of the Cheltenham Gold Cup, the Ebor Handicap, the Cambridgeshire and Cesarewitch, and the Tote Gold Trophy (formerly the Schweppes). And their profits go back into racing.

**Big Mac says . . .**

*Although the Tote is sometimes thought of as a medium for small punters rather than the big hitters, it's always worth keeping an eye on the Tote screens if you've come racing – and especially if you're interested in an outsider. The watchword always is to compare the prices: had you been perspicacious enough to choose Jet Ski Lady for the eight-runner 1991 Oaks and back her on the Tote, you'd not have been best pleased with the return of £16.50 – equivalent to 15½–1. Her returned starting price was 50–1. But when Jenny Pitman sent out Royal Athlete to land The Cuddly One her second Grand National in 1994, Tote backers had a return of £83.70 to a £1 stake, while backers at SP were rewarded with a comparatively measly 40–1, less than half the Tote odds.*

*You can't be definitive about when to back on the Tote, though as a rule Tote prices tend to be skinnier than the bookies' about an obviously popular runner – one owned by the Queen, for instance, or a horse who has captured the imagination like the greys Desert Orchid or the ill-fated One Man. Horses with sexy names, like Good In Bed or Virile Mac, or those ridden by star jockeys such as Frankie Dettori and Tony McCoy, attract the small-time punters, and they tend to favour the Tote's wonderful Ladies in Red over those fierce, intimidating bookmakers in the betting ring! That's one reason why the whole ethos of the jungle is being radically revised as racing heads into the millennium to make the arena far more consumer-friendly.*

## Tote betting

### Win

You bet on one horse to come first.

- The record win dividend was £341 2s 6d to a two-shilling stake on Coole at Haydock Park on 30 November 1929: the Tote odds of over 3,410–1 compared with a starting price of 100–8: just over 12–1.

### Place

You bet on a horse to be placed:

- first or second in races of five, six or seven runners;
- first, second or third in races of eight runners or more;
- first, second, third or fourth in handicaps of sixteen runners or more.

The record place dividend was £67.32 to 10p on Strip Fast (started 66–1), second in an apprentice race at Nottingham on 31 October 1978.

### Dual Forecast

In races of three or more runners, you pick two horses: you win if they finish first and second (in either order).

- The record dual forecast dividend was £4,609.40 to £1 in the opening race on Cesarewitch day at Newmarket, 15 October 1994 (starting prices 33–1 Chinour and 25–1 Royal Hill).

### Trifecta

The Trifecta is the Tote's most recent bet, introduced on the Vodafone Stewards' Cup at Goodwood on 1 August 1998. You pick the first three home in the designated race in correct order – simplicity itself! Although a punter could make just one selection of three horses to finish 1, 2, 3, most prefer permutations: to perm the finishing orders of three horses requires six bets, four horses twenty-four bets, five horses sixty bets, and so on.

The first Trifecta attracted a pool of £127,909, and the dividend for those gifted with second sight and nominating Superior Premium to beat Ansellman with Eastern Purple third was £6,311.00 to a £1 stake – compared with the bookmakers' Tricast on the same race paying £4,192.88.

### Jackpot

All you have to do is pick the winners of the first six races at the designated Jackpot meeting. If there is no winner the pool is carried forward to the next Jackpot meeting.

- The record Jackpot dividend was £273,365.80 to £1 at Newmarket on 2 October 1993.

### Placepot

You pick horses to be placed in the first six races (or, for any race with fewer than five runners, to win). The Placepot operates at all meetings.

- The record Placepot dividend was declared at Newmarket on 3 May 1998: £23,914.40 to a £1 stake.

### Quadpot

You pick horses to be placed in the final four legs of the Placepot.

- The record Quadpot dividend was £2,119.30 to £1 at Ascot on 15 June 1994.

**The year's big betting races**

The major bookmaking firms publish lists of the races which provide the greatest amount of betting turnover. For Ladbrokes, the largest bookmaker in Britain, the top twenty races in 1997, by turnover, were:

1 Martell Grand National (Aintree) – BBC
2 Vodafone Derby (Epsom Downs) – Channel Four
3 Tote Cheltenham Gold Cup (Cheltenham) – Channel Four
4 Vodac Stewards' Cup (Goodwood) – BBC
5 Pertemps Two Thousand Guineas (Newmarket) – Channel Four
6 Smurfit Champion Hurdle (Cheltenham) – Channel Four
7 Pertemps King George VI Chase (Kempton Park) – Channel Four
8 Worthington Lincoln Handicap (Doncaster) – Channel Four
9 Tote Cambridgeshire Handicap (Newmarket) – Channel Four
10 King George VI and Queen Elizabeth Diamond Stakes (Ascot) – BBC

Of these top ten, seven were shown live on Channel Four.

# Variations and complications

## Ante-post betting

Ante-post betting – wagering on an event well in advance of its taking place – provides the potential for lashings of value: provided, that is, that your selection actually gets to the start of the race.

Bets on the very big races – the Grand National, the first four Classics, the Cheltenham Gold Cup, Champion Hurdle and Triumph Hurdle – are being struck months before, while most of the big handicaps on the Flat (notably the Lincoln, Stewards' Cup, Cambridgeshire and Cesarewitch) attract lively markets for several weeks before they are actually run.

If you are exceptionally clairvoyant, you can even bet years in advance, provided you can get someone to take the bet. In 1967 the famous bookmaker William Hill laid owner Raymond Guest £50,000 to £500 (100–1) against an as yet unraced two-year-old winning the Derby the following year (and, for good measure, £12,500 to £500 the place): the horse was Sir Ivor, who won the Derby easily under Lester Piggott in 1968. The starting price was 5–4 on.

Another unraced two-year-old was the subject of a wondrous ante-post bet in 1986. Derek Powley, manager of the Cliveden Stud, got odds of 500–1 that a colt who had been foaled at the stud the previous year would win the 1987 Derby, and the horse did just that: Reference Point, starting price 6–4.

It can work the other way. In May 1986 a man walked into a West Country betting shop and asked for a price about an as yet unnamed four-month-old foal by Mill Reef out of 1983 Arc winner All Along winning the 1989 Derby. Quoted 500–1, he forked out £300 on the nose. Along All (as the foal was named) kept the punter's hope alive through an encouraging juvenile career in France, but never got to run in the 1989 Derby.

The great advantage of ante-post betting is of course that you can get very much better odds than the horse will start at – though this is not guaranteed: the horse's price may lengthen. The great disadvantage is that you lose your money if the horse is withdrawn before the race. (But note this: if your horse is withdrawn but the race is abandoned you get your money back, for you cannot lose on an event which does not happen.)

Sometimes bookmakers will offer ante-post odds 'with a run' – that is, if the horse does not take part your money is returned. All the 'Will she? Won't she?' speculation buzzing around Cape Verdi before her connections decided whether she would take on the colts in the 1998 Vodafone Derby meant that in the weeks between her One Thousand Guineas victory and the announcement that she would run she made an extremely dubious ante-post proposition, as the likelihood that she would miss the Derby and go instead for the more natural target the Vodafone Oaks remained live. Once it was decided that she would take on the colts, order was restored to the Derby ante-post market – but punters who had backed her for the Oaks before her mightily impressive win at Newmarket, many when she was a two-year-old, took great umbrage that she missed that race and thus denied them of the opportunity of a nice touch. That episode illustrates the inherent danger of ante-post betting – you simply don't know what is going to happen between your striking the bet and the race itself.

**Big Mac says . . .**

*Bookmakers claim that they lose on ante-post betting, and that it's principally window-dressing, but from the punter's point of view it can provide a great deal of fun. Even a poor man like me can have his moments, and the memory is still strong of how an ante-post voucher on Zafonic for the 1993 Two Thousand Guineas, acquired at Longchamp the day Khalid Abdullah's great colt romped away with the Prix de la Salamandre, gave me a rosy glow all that winter – and Zafonic did not let me down at Newmarket, charging home at 6–5 on, a good deal skinnier price than I had on my ante-post voucher. If only ante-post were always that straightforward!*

*But a few words of ante-post advice:*

- *Be wary of a long-distance ante-post punt on a horse whose chances might be diminished by extremes of going: you cannot tell far in advance that he'll have conditions in his favour on the day.*
- *Be careful about serious ante-post betting in a race where the draw is known to be a significant factor, such as the Lincoln Handicap or the Ayr Gold Cup.*
- *The more inside knowledge you have about running plans the better. Be as sure as you can be that the horse is actually being aimed at the race in question.*
- *Remember that wisest of old betting sayings: 'You can't go skint taking a profit.' If the horse you've backed ante-post at 50–1 shortens to 6–4 favourite, you could theoretically lay that horse at 2–1 yourself and be guaranteed a profit. Theoretically – but not legally, unless you have a bookmaker's licence. When you find yourself the happy possessor of a 50–1 voucher about a 6–4 chance, make the most of it by backing other horses in the race.*
- *Don't throw away your voucher as soon as the horse is withdrawn. If the race is abandoned (and even the Derby was threatened in 1983), all ante-post bets are refunded.*

### Betting tax

If you make a bet off-course – say in a betting shop – you will be liable to a tax (usually 9 per cent) on the transaction. Tax can be

- added to your stake – so that a £5 bet 'tax paid' would actually cost you £5.45 but you would have no deduction from your returns in the event of winning; or

- deducted from your return (that is, winnings plus returned stake): so if you had a £5 winning bet at 10–1 and did not bet 'tax paid', handing over just the fiver, your actual return – the amount you would collect – would be £50.95 (£50 winnings plus £5 stake less £4.95, 9 per cent of the total).

You pays your money and you takes your choice, but it is worth being aware of the effect of tax on very short-priced winners. A £10 winning bet at evens, without tax paid at the time of making the bet, returns £18.20, a profit on the transaction of just £8.20. The same bet tax paid on would return a profit of £9.10 – work it out! A bet of £10 to win, tax not paid on, which comes in at 2–1 on brings a return of just £13.65. Remember that the same bet on-course, where there is no betting tax, would give you a return of £15.

## Rule 4

Betting is regulated by rules laid down by the Tattersalls Committee. Rule 4 addresses the problem of the distortions in the betting market which occur if one (or more) of the runners is withdrawn shortly before the race – for example, when a horse refuses to enter the starting stalls: betting will have started in earnest on that race and there may be no time to make a new book. In such instances, money staked on the horse withdrawn is returnable to the punters. The shorter the price of that horse at the time of withdrawal, the greater the distortion of the market, so Rule 4 sets out a scale whereby a deduction is made from all winning bets in that race, the size of the deduction depending on the price of the withdrawn horse at the time of withdrawal.

Rule 4 also applies when a horse is deemed by the starter not to have taken part in the race – for instance, if a horse whips round at a tape start and refuses to race.

The scale of deductions is as follows:

| Price | Deduction (p in the £) |
|---|---|
| 30–100 (or shorter) | 75 |
| 2–5 to 1–3 | 70 |
| 8–15 to 4–9 | 65 |
| 8–13 to 4–7 | 60 |
| 4–5 to 4–6 | 55 |
| 20–21 to 5–6 | 50 |
| evens to 6–5 | 45 |
| 5–4 to 6–4 | 40 |
| 13–8 to 7–4 | 35 |
| 15–8 to 9–4 | 30 |
| 5–2 to 3–1 | 25 |
| 100–30 to 4–1 | 20 |
| 9–2 to 11–2 | 15 |
| 6–1 to 9–1 | 10 |
| 10–1 to 14–1 | 5 |
| 15–1 and over | no deduction |

## Dead heat

In the case of a dead heat the punter receives the full odds to half the stake. So £5 to win on a horse which started at 10–1 and dead-heated for first place would return (forgetting tax) £27.50 – winnings of £25 plus the return of half the stake (£2.50).

## No starting price

When Dancing Brave turned out for his Arc prep race at Goodwood in September 1986 he was such a total, stone-bonking certainty to beat his five opponents that course bookmakers could muster no interest in betting on the result of the race. When such races happen (they occasionally do) no starting prices are returned. All bets struck are void.

## Spread betting

Fixed-odds betting, however baffling it may appear at first sight to the uninitiated, is simplicity itself compared with spread betting. This novel form of punting, pioneered by companies such as Sporting Index and City Index, has grown rapidly throughout the 1990s and is now an integral part of the betting scene.

The essence of spread betting is wagering on a range – a 'spread' – of possibilities. Most sporting events are decided by numbers – runs in cricket, goals in soccer, points in rugby – and the spread better backs his or her view on what those numbers will be. So if the spread-betting firm is of the opinion that the total number of points scored in a rugby international will be 29, it may quote '28–30'. If you think the match will produce more points than 29, you 'buy' at 30; if fewer than 29, you 'sell' at 28. The punter makes the decision to buy (the higher figure) or sell (the lower) and stipulates the stake, but here's the rub: your profit or loss on the bet is calculated by measuring the difference between the price at which you bought or sold and the actual result, and multiplying your stake by that figure. So, unlike in fixed-odds betting, your losses are not confined to the amount you have staked. If you buy the spread at £10 and the total number of points is 25, you lose £50: 30 minus 25 equals 5. But if you sell the spread at £10 and the total number of points is 25, you win £30 (28 minus 25).

Interesting, but what has this to do with horse racing? Applications of spread betting in racing have included such matters as

- how many runners will complete the course in the Grand National;
- the total winning distances at an individual race meeting;
- performances of favourites at a meeting, with market leaders scoring points on an advertised scale;
- the distance by which one named horse will beat another, wherever they actually finish in the race.

As with fixed-odds betting, the spread changes with circumstances – and, in the case of most sports, during the event itself.

## Spread betting on the 1998 Derby

As an example of how spread betting applies to horse racing, this is the spread advertised by Ladbrokes on the morning of the 1998 Vodafone Derby at Epsom:

| | | |
|---|---|---|
| Greek Dance | 19–22 | |
| Cape Verdi | 13–16 | |
| Second Empire | 12–15 | |
| City Honours | 8–11 | |
| Gulland | 6–8 | |
| Saratoga Springs | 6–8 | |
| Courteous | 5–7 | |
| Haami | 5–7 | |
| King Of Kings | 5–7 | winner 50 points |
| The Glow Worm | 5–7 | second 30 points |
| Border Arrow | 4–6 | third 20 points |
| High-Rise | 4–6 | fourth 10 points |
| Sadian | 3–5 | |
| Mutamam | 1–3 | |
| Sunshine Street | 0.1–1 | |

Say you 'bought' Greek Dance for £10. The colt finished fifth, so you lose 22 times your stake: £220. Had he won, you would, on the scale of points advertised, have netted 28 (50 points for winning, less the 22 of the spread) times your stake: £280. Had he come second, you would have won £80. Had he come third, you would have lost £20 (22 minus 20 equals 2). On the other hand, had you taken a dim view of Greek Dance's chance, figuring that he would finish unplaced, you could have 'sold' him, in which case a £10 unit would have won you £190 – 19 times your stake. Had you 'bought' the winner High-Rise for £10, you would have won £440 (50 minus 6 equals 44, times your stake).

To illustrate the perils and possibilities of spread betting, compare the Greek Dance spread bet with what would have happened had you had a tenner on the colt at his starting price of 5–1: maximum loss £10, possible winnings £50.

One of the attractions of spread betting is that you can back your opinion if you think the horse in question will lose, as well as if you think he will win. Another is that the more right you are, the more money you will win. The danger, of course, is that the more wrong you are, the more you will lose (though in bets such as those relating to distance a ceiling is usually imposed).

Two other points to remember. You cannot have a spread bet in a betting shop or on the racecourse – only through an account with one of the spread bookmakers. And if you get it so comprehensively wrong that you cannot afford to pay up, beware: unlike with orthodox betting, you can be sued for the debt by your bookmaker. (And he, should it come to it, can be sued by you.)

### Betting on overseas races

Time was when the only occasion a British punter might think about having a bet on an overseas race was on the first Sunday in October, and the perennial question would come up: is it better to back your fancy for the Prix de l'Arc de Triomphe at odds advertised by the bookies at home, or go for the on-track price offered by the Pari-Mutuel – the French tote monopoly?

Nowadays racing is increasingly international, with British horses regularly making forays to the top races abroad – not only in France and Ireland, but further afield in North America (where the Breeders' Cup has transformed the shape of the racing year), Dubai, Japan and even Australia (whose Melbourne Cup is now frequently a target for adventurous British and Irish trainers).

Bookmakers will usually advertise prices about the major overseas races – in some cases, such as the Arc, there will be a lively ante-post market – so the punter has a choice between taking those prices or betting at the locally returned prices, which are usually (as in France or the United States) Pari-Mutuel or tote prices.

The difference between bookmakers' and Pari-Mutuel prices can be spectacular. When Tolomeo – trained at Newmarket by Luca Cumani and ridden by Pat Eddery – won the Arlington Million in Chicago in 1983 he was priced as low as 6–1 by British layers, but the horse was little known in America and paid 38.2–1 on the track.

Such bonanza payouts are becoming rarer as overseas punters get more used to seeing British raiders in their races, and today there is less likelihood of a horse with a real chance being ignored in the local betting: when Dancing Brave ran in the Breeders' Cup Turf at Santa Anita in 1986, he went off the 2–1 on favourite – but still lost.

## Lays and Bismarcks

Since betting on horses is essentially a matter of pitching the punter's opinion against the bookmaker's, it is an invaluable part of the punting armoury to be able to second-guess the bookie. If you know that he is willing to 'lay' a horse, to take money for that runner in the expectation that it will not win, you will want to know why – and take his opposition either as a warning signal or as an opportunity for some decent value.

John McCririck's 'Lay of the Day', begun in early 1998 and intended to highlight fancied horses who should be opposed, merely turned up an embarrassing succession of winners, culminating in Martin Pipe's Blowing Wind, 5–1 favourite when landing the Sunderlands Imperial Cup at Sandown Park in March. Having kissed the feet of trainer Martin Pipe in the Sandown winner's enclosure, Big Mac announced the early demise of Lay of the Day: 'I keep on saying I'm a man who can hardly tip a loser, so I'm out of it now. It just shows why I'm a failed bookmaker.'

Cue a real professional in the shape of bookmaker Barry Dennis. Barry's weekly telephonic presence on *The Morning Line* (occasionally dripping straight from the shower) became a feature of the Saturday morning show, and an invaluable insight into how a top bookmaker assesses a race. For example, two of the leading fancies for the 1998 Vodafone Derby were nominated as 'Barry's Bismarcks' despite strong support in the ante-post market – and sure enough, neither Cape Verdi nor Greek Dance reached the frame.

In weighing up a race, it's as vital to know why individual horses might not win as why they might.

## Betting on sport – and beyond

Few punters confine themselves purely to horse racing (or horses and greyhounds), and the last few years have seen a huge increase in the level of sports betting: the 1998 World Cup in France was described as 'the planet's biggest betting event' by Graham Sharpe of William Hill; industry-wide, the competition reportedly produced a betting turnover of £120 million. It also, again according to William Hill, twice broke the record for the biggest bet ever placed: one punter had £200,000 on England to beat Colombia at 5–4 on (thereby winning £160,000), and the same high-roller had £240,000 on Brazil to beat France in the final (thereby returning his earlier winnings – and more).

There has also been a surge in betting on non-sporting outcomes, such as political events – and other contests. When in 1990 senior clerics entered the stalls for the race to be next Archbishop of Canterbury, George Carey started out the 20–1 'rag', then attracted suspiciously heavy betting just before the off: Ladbrokes took £2,000 for him on the very morning of the announcement. Carey duly came in, whereupon dark rumours started circulating that the bookmakers had been stitched up by insiders in the know . . .

Then there is a wholly daft vein of betting which attracts huge media attention on account of its sheer zaniness. At the end of August 1998, William Hill would lay you

- 10,000–1 that a UFO will land on top of the Millennium Dome at Greenwich some time during the year 2000;
- 2,000–1 that Elvis Presley will be proved to be still alive;
- 500–1 a positive sighting of the Loch Ness Monster.

But even these bets are not as bizarre as that sought by the punter who some years ago contacted Ron Pollard, Ladbrokes' renowned odds guru, and asked for a price about the actress Mae West being shown on her death to have been a man all along.

# Getting on

There are three ways to place a bet on a horse race:

- on the racecourse;
- in a betting shop;
- through an account with a bookmaker.

## On the racecourse

'Five to four the field . . . I'll lay six to four . . . sixes bar one . . .'

Bookmakers shouting the odds provide a British racecourse with its unique sound, a babble of noise which at first may sound like gibberish but on closer attention reveals business being transacted swiftly between layers and punters.

When a bookmaker shouts 'five to four the field' (which usually sounds like 'fidah vaudeville') he – very rarely she – is indicating that 5–4 is the shortest price he has on offer; 'I'll take six to four' means he is offering 6–4 on, while 'I'll lay six to four' means 6–4 against; 'sixes bar one' means that he is offering all the runners in the race except one at 6–1 or longer.

The principal betting ring at most racecourses is in 'Tatts' – the Tattersalls enclosure, named after the company which in 1866 drew up the first rules on betting transactions. (The Tattersalls Committee is still recognized as the body with authority to settle all disputes relating to bets, and has the power to 'warn off' – that is, ban from racecourses – an individual for non-payment.)

Betting with bookmakers is not usually allowed in the Members' enclosure, so the larger companies have representatives who maintain a position by the rail dividing Members from Tatts, and take bets – some in cash, many in credit – from the members on the other side of it. Much of the serious punting is done here with these 'rails bookmakers'. In the main betting ring bookmakers are allotted pitches according to seniority; here they set up shop with a clerk (who records the bets on a large ledger or 'field book' – one column per runner, so that the liability on any horse can be rapidly assessed if need be) and other assistants and tic-tac men. The bookmaker himself will handle the money, shovelling it into (and occasionally out of) a large bag suspended from his stand. In case of disputes over bets, many course layers position a small tape recorder beneath their board to provide aural confirmation of bets recorded in writing in the ledger, and modern microchip technology is now allowing the use of laptop computers which will print out a formal statement of the bet, rather than the coloured ticket which has traditionally been the punter's sole record of the transaction.

Having begun betting from the 'tissue', the course bookmaker adjusts the odds according to the flow of money until the race is started, at which point two official starting price reporters agree on what is to be the officially returned starting price (SP) for each horse. To arrive at these, they note the prices available all round the ring, and if there are significant discrepancies will often split the difference. So if approximately a quarter of the significant layers have the favourite at 5–4 at the off, half are offering 6–5 and others go 11–10 or evens the same horse, the officially returned starting price is likely to be 6–5. The same process explains weird SPs like 85–40 (halfway between 2–1 and 9–4).

Some people are put off betting in the ring by the sheer level of activity – all that hustle and bustle as punters search around for the best price, then panic as they see it start to go before they've got on, and push and shove to get to the last bookie showing those odds – only to see him wipe it off the board just as they reach his pitch. ('It's on my finger' has sometimes been the snide retort, while wiping the chalk away on his trousers.) But the brave are rewarded with the fun of being part of that seething mass of activity, and the actual trans-action is perfectly straightforward.

The bookmaker displays his odds on a board, constantly revising them as the market shifts by wiping them off and writing up fresh ones. When you see a bookmaker showing against the name of your fancy the price you want to bet at, go up, offer the money and state the bet you want. So if you're going to have five pounds to win on High-Rise and the bookie is showing High-Rise at 20–1, simply say: '£5 to win High-Rise', or, better still, ' £100 to £5 High-Rise'. He will call the bet to his clerk as 'a hundred to five High-Rise' (that is, your bet is £100 to £5) and give you a small numbered ticket which is your receipt for that wager – or, at the most ultra-modern pitches, a computerised receipt which actually states your bet. The clerk notes the bet in his 'field book', and to avoid possible confusion you should make a note of the bet struck on the back of the ticket. After High-Rise has won, you return to the bookmaker and hand him your ticket: he will relay the number on it to his clerk, who will confirm the payout – and before you know it your fiver will have become £105 in your pocket, and you will be about to make new friends.

The main on-course alternative to betting with a bookmaker is to bet with the Tote. This is an altogether more orderly experience. You join a queue leading up to any Tote window, and while queuing make sure you know the number – not the name – of your selection. On reaching the window, state that number (or numbers), the type of bet you want (see pages 70–1 above) and the amount to be staked, and hand over your money. You will be given a receipt for your bet (which you should check before leaving the window, as even the Tote's famous Ladies in Red are fallible). If you win, return to any Tote window – it doesn't have to be the one where you placed the bet – present your ticket, and you'll be paid. Simple!

**Big Mac says . . .**

*Come racing!*

*At last, the betting jungle is becoming customer-friendly, caring, like all progressive businesses.*

*Look what you get:*

- *No betting tax – you'll be paying 9 per cent off-course.*
- *The chance to bet at the very last minute, when you've been able to study the runners at close quarters in the paddock, watch them go down to the start, absorb all the clues and pick up racecourse gossip.*
- *The opportunity to shop around for the best prices in the betting ring.*
- *Betting without the favourite, in running, on photo finishes, stewards' enquiries and so on*
- *The chance (not available in a shop) to 'take the fractions' and bet £25 to £4, rather than 6–1, or 100–6 rather than 16–1. Most course bookmakers will offer the 'fracs' – and if one won't, just go elsewhere.*

*I don't wish to repeat myself, but . . .*
   *Come racing!*

## Betting shops

Today there are about 8,000 betting shops in Britain, responsible for a large proportion of the £5,000 million bet off-course every year. Forty years ago there weren't any at all. Until 1 May 1961, when the first betting shops in Great Britain were opened, betting on horses could legally be done only on a racecourse or through a credit account. Illegally, it was done all over the place, with 'bookies' runners' operating in pubs and clubs and on street corners; and it was in an attempt to stamp out this illicit activity that Home Secretary R. A. 'Rab' Butler introduced the Betting and Gaming Act that made betting shops possible.

   Legal was one thing; attractive was another entirely. Butler noted in his memoirs that 'the House of Commons was so intent on making betting shops as sad as possible, in order not to deprave the young, that they ended up more like undertakers' premises'. Indeed, for decades betting shops laboured under a reputation as seedy and uninviting places fostered by the regulations on their operation – they were not allowed to show races live on television or offer light refreshments to their patrons; but after a couple of decades of stumbling on in the gloom, a less censorious approach won through.

New legislation passed in 1986 allowed a general brightening up of betting shops and, most significantly, the transmission of races live on television from Satellite Information Services. Even coffee machines appeared. At last, the notion of a betting shop as an establishment into which no respectable person should ever stray unless under extreme duress, in which case the experience should be as shaming and uncomfortable as possible to discourage its repetition, had at last disappeared. Now, with evening opening and Sunday opening, betting shops have become respectable outposts of the leisure industry, a move accelerated early in 1995 when they were at last allowed to show their interiors to high-street passers-by, rather than skulking guiltily behind solid display boards in the shop windows.

Nevertheless, despite their more inviting demeanour these days, to some folk betting shops still have the magnetic but intimidating aura of the brothel; so, for would-be clients still shy about entering such a place, it may be helpful to explain how you have a bet.

Around the walls are displayed a large array of newspapers and television screens giving all sorts of information on the day's sport. When you've decided what you want to back, take a carbon-backed slip from one of the dispensers on the counters all round the shop – different sorts of bet require different slips – and write on it the details of your bet. (Ballpoint pens are thoughtfully provided for the purpose.) It is essential that you fill in this slip accurately: if you had got confused and had a fiver on High Honours in the 1998 Derby (when High-Rise beat City Honours) you would have had no right to feel aggrieved if the bookmaker called the bet void, and all sorts of disputes arise from wrongly or ambiguously filled-in slips, or slips placing some highly elaborate combination wager when the amount staked does not cover the bets involved.

The slip itself is not very difficult. For a win bet you would just need to enter the name of the horse, the time of the race and the course where it is to be run, and the amount you wish to stake. (You also have the option to have the bet 'tax paid', which means that you pay the betting tax on the stake: see page 75.) You give the slip and your money to the assistant behind the counter, who will time-stamp the slip in a machine and return the bottom copy to you. You then, according to your constitution, either hang around nonchalantly as your horse sweeps to victory on the screen or scurry off to shout and perspire in the privacy of your own home, and when the 'weighed-in' signal is given saunter to the payout end of the counter to collect your winnings.

Remember that if you have not bet 'tax paid' 9 per cent will be taken off your returns – that is, your winnings and your returned stake; but betting tax does not apply to bets struck with a bookmaker on the racecourse.

## Accounts

If you're going to bet off-course, you can give yourself a much more leisurely time of it by opening an account with a bookmaker. No more scuttling down to the betting shop during the adverts or placing all your bets in advance of the afternoon's transmission; you can bet by telephone at the very last minute, enabling you to make full use of the wisdom of the Channel Four Racing team as they discuss the runners in each race and to form your own judgements of how the horses behave in the preliminaries and go down to the start before you commit yourself.

It is easy to open an account: all the major credit firms advertise in the racing press. You'll need to decide what sort of account you want – whether a deposit account, whereby you deposit a sum of money with the bookmaker (probably not less than £100 with the big firms) and can bet until that amount is used up, or a credit account, where you are allowed credit up to an agreed limit. The introduction of accounts using Switch cards makes the debit of money from your bank account – when you lose – immediate, so you won't be building up huge debts.

You will be sent a statement regularly – very occasionally this will be accompanied by a cheque – and you can use your credit account with these firms' representatives at race meetings: Tote Credit, with 50,000 clients, has a special office on all courses.

# Systems

Betting systems provide a sort of template for your punting, a framework that dictates how and when you put your money on. Not many people bet only according to a system, but most regular punters have a few schemes they like to bear in mind, from supposedly logical notions such as backing the top weight in a nursery (a handicap for two-year-olds), on the basis that it is demonstrably the best horse in the race, to wholly illogical ones such as betting on greys or on a horse whose racecard number coincides with the date of Granny's birthday.

Among the most regularly followed systems are:

- backing favourites (around a third of all races are won by the market leader, but you won't make a profit out of backing them blindly);
- blindly backing horses ridden by a particular jockey (sometimes it works, sometimes it doesn't, as the case of phenomenal National Hunt champion Tony McCoy illustrates: had you had a £1 bet on every one of his 831 rides in the 1997–8 season you would have backed 253 winners but ended up £20.60 down);
- backing particular trainers at particular courses – e.g. Martin Pipe at any of the West Country tracks.

Our Man In The Ring, never one to be a slave to a system, marks your card . . .

## Big Mac's top dozen systems

*If there were a system that worked, everyone would have twigged by now. But it does no harm to have a few which might throw up the odd winner, and these are the ones I would recommend:*

- *Back the horse that won the same race last year. Many of the relevant factors – type of race, course, distance, time of year – are in its favour.*
- *Back horses blinkered or visored for the first time.*
- *Back the outsider of three. There's more logic to this than might be apparent at first, as races with very small fields are often run at a false pace, making a less predictable result more likely, and when punters concentrate on the first two in the betting there may be value to be had from the outsider.*
- *If a top jockey is riding at his absolute minimum weight, back his horse. He wouldn't have given up even his meagre breakfast if the creature had no chance!*
- *In handicaps, restrict yourself to horses running off their old mark when their new rating will be higher. (See page 41.) They are clearly improving, and should be caught before their official reassessment is dictating the weight they carry.*
- *In amateur and apprentice races, go for the most experienced and best jockey, whatever he or she is riding.*
- *Consider the effect of the draw sensibly. If a race is run on extremes of going and the draw has a marked effect, concentrate on the favoured side for all bets, including forecasts.*
- *When studying a maiden race, find out whether any of the runners are engaged in big races later in the season: those that are must be highly rated by connections.*
- *Back the animal whose stable has sent it the longest distance for the race.*
- *If a stable has more than one runner in a race, go for the outsider. They won't come in too often, but when they do rewards can be great. Think of Godolphin second string*

*Cape Cross winning the 1998 Lockinge Stakes at Newbury at 20–1 with the first string Kahal, ridden by Frankie Dettori, back in fourth place.*
- *Totally illogically, support horses with the same initials in forecasts.*
- *And, just as bad, go for any horse whose racecard number is the same as its starting stall position.*

*But never get hooked on a system. It removes the flexibility – and a lot of the fun – from your punting. And whatever you do, don't forget that telegram wired home by the roulette player: 'System working well – send more money!'*

# Winners and losers

While it is impossible to be precise about exactly how much is wagered on a particular horse, some bets have become fabled.

## Catching them early

Here are a couple of cases to inspire Channel Four Racing viewers thinking of having a cool twenty thou on their fancy:

### Nashwan in the 1989 Two Thousand Guineas

Available at 33–1 only a few weeks before the race after an encouraging but not earth-shattering two-year-old career, Nashwan was backed steadily as reports came out of trainer Dick Hern's yard that the imposing chestnut had turned in a phenomenal gallop. In the words of Brough Scott in the *Racing Post*, 'all sorts of quite sane and sensible people around the Hern camp began to mutter behind their hands and shake at the knees.' They managed to control those knees enough to wobble down to the betting shop, and by the day of the race Nashwan's price had tumbled: Ladbrokes alone laid the colt to lose £250,000. Starting 3–1 favourite, Nashwan devoured the Rowley Mile to win from Exbourne and then go on to land the Derby at 5–4.

The bookies may consider accumulators 'mugs' bets', but in May 1995 a lady pensioner in Nottingham begged to differ. She staked a five pence accumulator on five horses, and for good measure added a Super Flag (a multiple bet of baffling complexity) on the same quintet. The result . . .

- Christian Flight won at 20–1
- Don't Forget Ruby won at 12–1
- Romany Creek won at 20–1
- Groomsman won at 66–1
- How's It Goin won at 7–1

The accumulated winning odds of 3,072,887–1 were reported by Ladbrokes, who laid the bet, as a world record, and the punter's winnings came to £208,098.79 for an outlay of just over £5.

Some mug!

### Pasternak in the 1997 Cambridgeshire

Best-priced 11–1 on the morning of the race, Pasternak, trained by Sir Mark Prescott, was the subject of a major gamble, opening at 9–2 in the Newmarket betting ring before being sent off half a point shorter at 4–1. His victory over stable companion Rudimental reputedly cost the bookmakers £5 million.

## Expensive failures

### Dancing Brave in the 1986 Derby

After a storming victory in the Two Thousand Guineas, Dancing Brave was the subject of a massive gamble for the Derby and went off 2–1 favourite despite doubts about his stamina. Those same doubts dictated jockey Greville Starkey's tactics, with the horse being kept in the rear of the field. Third last at Tattenham Corner, he started to make up ground in the straight, but Shahrastani had gone beyond recall, and at the post Dancing Brave was still half a length short of the lead. Burnt fingers all round.

### The Fellow in the 1993 Cheltenham Gold Cup

Short-headed for steeplechasing's most prestigious prize in both 1991 and 1992, The Fellow was reportedly the most heavily backed horse in the history of the Gold Cup when going off 5–4 favourite; the recorded on-course bets alone included

£22,000 to £16,000
£10,500 to £6,000
£7,000 to £4,000 (four times)
£6,500 to £4,000 (twice)
£12,000 to £8,000
£7,500 to £5,000
£6,000 to £4,000 (twice)

Serious stuff; but The Fellow could finish only fourth behind Jodami. Twelve months later he rewarded loyalists by winning at 7–1.

---

The longest ever starting price returned about a winner in Britain was 250–1 about Equinoctial, winner of the Grants Whisky Novices' Hurdle at Kelso on 21 November 1990.

---

### Gaelic Storm in the 1998 Stewards' Cup

The manic rush to get on Gaelic Storm for the Vodafone Stewards' Cup at Goodwood on 1 August 1998 was a prime example of the bandwagon effect – and then some.

Generally available earlier in the week at 20–1, Gaelic Storm started to attract punters' attention in the couple of days before the race as it became apparent that his trainer Mark Johnston was in top form. On the Friday – the eve of the Stewards' Cup – the wheels of the bandwagon started to turn gently, and then picked up speed considerably after the horse was recommended by one of the major telephone tipping services.

By the morning of the race Gaelic Storm had become a huge steamer – to the extent that the 16–1 still available with some firms first thing soon halved. He opened in the on-course market at 6–1 favourite before easing to a starting price of 8–1, joint market leader.

Bookmakers' liabilities were running at several million pounds by the time the stalls for the Stewards' Cup slammed open; but Gaelic Storm did not let them down, finishing fifteenth of the twenty-nine runners.

---

In April 1993 Countess Crossett was chalked up in the ring at Kelso at 5,000–1, thought to be the longest price ever laid on a British racecourse. She started at a mere 500–1 and finished ninth of seventeen.

---

## Flying the coup

Nashwan and Pasternak are examples of bets which are often described as 'coups' – large-scale successful bets brought about by astute planning – but in both cases there was a significant bandwagon effect, with the horse's price continuing to shrink when the betting public is alerted to what is going on and rushes to get in on the action.

Often a coup will be brought about by the horse being carefully prepared for a race in such a way that the bookmakers have a less accurate idea of its chance than those who are betting on it, and will consequently let it be backed at an over-generous price; the history of the Turf is peppered with occasions when a massive amount of money invested has caused a dramatic reduction in the odds of a horse.

But the coup which pushes against – and sometimes through – the bounds of legality is easier to pull off in a small race which will attract little attention, and the most sensational frauds of the post-war era have taken place in minor events.

### Francasal

A selling race at Bath on 16 July 1953 was won by a horse named Francasal at 10–1; but investigations revealed that the winner was not Francasal but a 'ringer' – a horse of similar appearance but different ability, in this case a much faster animal named Santa Amaro. The main perpetrators of the affair were convicted and gaoled.

### Flockton Grey

Suspicions were aroused when Flockton Grey won a two-year-old maiden race at Leicester in March 1982 at 10–1, not least because he won so easily – by twenty lengths. The horse turned out to be the three-year-old Good Hand. Again, those who had masterminded the coup ended up in court, and Flockton Grey himself spent years in police custody: he was subsequently co-owned by Michael Aspel.

### Gay Future

Perhaps the most ingenious stroke of all was the Gay Future affair: planned in Ireland, prepared in Scotland, and culminating in Cumbria, at Cartmel on August Bank Holiday 1974.

The architects of the coup had sent an unnamed horse to the stables of trainer Anthony Collins at Troon in Scotland. Collins had entered a horse called Gay Future and another horse, Racionzer, in the race at Cartmel, and two other horses – Opera Cloak and Ankerwyke – in races at other courses on the same day, both starting within half an hour of the Cartmel race. On that Bank Holiday morning, 26 August, members of the syndicate who were staging the coup placed bets in a variety of betting shops in London: doubles connecting Gay Future with Opera Cloak or with Ankerwyke. Doubles are deemed by bookmakers to be 'mugs' bets', and betting in small amounts in this manner would not have aroused suspicion.

Meanwhile the real Gay Future, who had been prepared for his race in Ireland, had been brought over the Irish Sea, swapped for the horse in Collins's charge, and sent off to Cartmel to run in the Ulverston Novices' Hurdle. Neither Ankerwyke nor Opera Cloak reached the courses where they were supposed to be running; indeed, it transpired later that they had never left their trainer's stable.

When one leg of a double is a non-runner the bet becomes a single on the remaining horse, so the failure of the other two horses to show meant that a large amount of money was now running on Gay Future; but the 'blower' system which transmits off-course money to the course betting market was not operating to Cartmel on that very busy Bank Holiday Monday (as the planners of the coup had cleverly been aware), and by the time the bookmakers – with no mobile phones in those days – realized what was afoot the only way they could get his price down was to send a representative to the course to bet on him there. The bookies' man did not arrive in time.

Before he had entered the paddock at Cartmel, Gay Future's flanks had had soap flakes rubbed into them to give the impression that he was sweating freely and so put off on-course punters, keeping the price up. The horse played his own part in the coup by strolling home fifteen lengths in front of his rivals at 10–1. Most of the betting shops who had taken the bets withheld payment, though some later regarded the matter as a legitimate coup and paid out. (The conspirators stood to win around £300,000.)

The police launched a prosecution; Collins and Tony Murphy, the Irish building contractor who was the main brain behind the coup, were convicted of conspiracy to defraud the bookmakers, and fined.

Whether or not the matter should have been brought to court was a question hotly debated at the time; whatever the legality or illegality of the episode, the Gay Future affair was certainly a coup of remarkable cunning and ingenuity.

---

The race with the most open betting ever was the 1964 Grand National, when Flying Wild, Laffy, Pappageno's Cottage and Time were co-favourites at 100–7.

---

## Sayings of the big hitters

Many gallons of printers' ink have been poured into the attempt to divine the secrets of those few legendary figures who have made their betting pay in spectacular fashion. Understandably, they tend to be sparing with their guidance; but here are a few words of wisdom from three of the great backers of horses which even the humblest punter might find worth pondering.

*J. P. McManus* is a legendary Irish punter and owner of many good racehorses including 1998 Champion Hurdle winner Istabraq (on which horse there was a single bet of £130,000 to win £80,000 – 13–8 on – in the Martell Aintree Hurdle on Grand National Day 1998: Istabraq was beaten a head by Pridwell) . . .

Racing is a great leveller. The day you think you have mastered the game, you will be made to pay for it the following day. What you must do is build up a bank of experience that allows you to reduce and eliminate as far as possible the factors that make for foolish betting. In a word, you act to strict ground rules always and you endeavour to become an investor rather than a pure addictive gambler.

*Barney Curley* – owner, trainer, famed gambler – was the brains behind the Yellow Sam coup at Bellewstown in Ireland in 1975, when the single telephone in the village was commandeered by an associate, thus preventing off-course money carefully bet on the horse getting into the on-course market. 'There was this heavily built man,' according to Curley himself, 'a tough sort of guy, who suddenly discovered that a close relation of his was seriously ill and he had to keep in constant touch with the hospital. Once he had the phone in his hand he was not going to let go. He was broad enough in the beam not to permit anyone past him into the box.' Yellow Sam pulled off a major touch by winning at a starting price of 20–1 – though in running you could only get 2–1! . . .

Professionals *never* bet on the six races on the card simply for the sake of having a bet. They don't see the last race as the 'getting out' stakes, should they be behind at that point. They will bring the shutters down if their main bet of the day on one of the earlier races is a losing one and look forward to the next day or their next opportunity to apply their judgement of form and the homework they will have to put in. They know that their knowledge must inevitably pay off once they can control their emotions and not chase losses.

And when *Phil Bull*, founder of Timeform and one of the best brains racing has ever known, was asked for Ten Commandments to accompany an article about him in the *Daily Telegraph* magazine in 1970, he wrote two versions – one of which serves as a checklist for all punters . . .

Seek where thou wilt for winners, but bet only when thou seest value; deliver thyself from the temptation to bet in every race.

Put not thy faith in luck, nor the law of averages, nor thy trust in staking systems, for these are delusions.

Let thy stake be related to the depth of thy pocket and to what thou regardest as the true chance of the horse; that which hath the greater chance deserveth the greater stake.

Thou shalt not bet each-way in big fields, unless thou art well satisfied as to the value of the place bet.

Bet with Book or Tote according to thy judgement: thus shalt thou endeavour to get the best of both worlds.

Thou shalt not bet ante-post except upon horses that are known to be definite runners.

Beware the man who would sell thee a system; if thou knowest a profitable one, preserve it to thyself in silence.

Double and treble if you must; but bet not upon objections, for thou hast not the evidence and the stewards know not what they do.

Let thy betting be informed by wisdom and diligence, and tempered by patience and caution, and leavened but a little with boldness.

Let thy bets be well within thy means: he that maketh his fortune in a week loseth his ducats in a day.

Amen to that!

# A Betting Dictionary

The peculiar language of betting adds to its mystique; like any language, it is easier to handle once you've learned a few basic terms. Here are a few of the commonest.

As well as definitions and explanations, the list below includes some of the slang terms used to describe odds, amounts of money, horses and other aspects of the betting operation: for some words and phrases the derivation is reasonably obvious, but others are more obscure.

*Accumulator* A bet involving several horses, where the returns from each winning selection are staked on the next.

*Across the card* Used of races run at the same time at different meetings.

*Ante-post* Betting well in advance of the event.

*Any to come* A term indicating that the whole or part of the returns of one bet are to be reinvested on another: for example, '£10 win Intikhab, any to come £5 win High-Rise' involves an initial stake of £10, with the subsequent bet being struck only if there are returns from the first.

*Bar* If a betting show is concluded '20–1 bar' it means that the horses not listed stand at 20–1 or longer.

*Beeswax* Betting tax.

### The odds in slang

For ease of reference, should you wish to communicate with your book-maker in betting slang, here are the odds in slang, arranged in order:

| | |
|---|---|
| evens | levels (variants: one to one and Scotch) |
| 11–10 | tips (variant: bits) |
| 6–5 | sais a ching |
| 5–4 | wrist (variant: hand to rouf) |
| 11–8 | up the arm |
| 6–4 | ear 'ole (variant: exes to rouf) |
| 13–8 | bits on the ear 'ole |
| 7–4 | shoulder (variant: neves to rouf) |
| 15–8 | double taps |
| 2–1 | bottle |
| 9–4 | top of the head (variant: enin to rouf) |
| 5–2 | face (variant: bottle and a half) |
| 11–4 | elef a vier |
| 3–1 | carpet (variants: tres and gimmel) |
| 100–30 | Burlington Bertie (variant: scruffy and dirty) |
| 7–2 | carpet and a half |
| 4–1 | rouf (variant: quat) |
| 9–2 | on the shoulders (variant: rouf and a half) |
| 5–1 | hand (variant: ching) |
| 11–2 | hand and a half (variant: ching and a half) |
| 6–1 | exes |
| 13–2 | exes and a half |
| 7–1 | neves |
| 15–2 | neves and a half |
| 8–1 | T.H. |
| 9–1 | enin |
| 10–1 | net (variant: cockle) |
| 11–1 | elef |
| 12–1 | net and bice |
| 14–1 | net and rouf |
| 16–1 | net and ex |
| 20–1 | score (variants: apple core and double net) |
| 25–1 | pony (variant: macaroni) |
| 33–1 | double carpet |

*Bogey* The horse which represents the biggest liability in a bookmaker's book.

*Board price* The price relayed to betting shops during the pre-race market moves and displayed there on the board: a punter can take this price and be on at those odds, regardless of starting price.

*Bottle* 2–1.

*Burlington Bertie* 100–30 (rhyming slang).

*Carpet* 3–1.

*Century* £100.

*Cockle* £10, or 10–1.

*Double carpet* 33–1.

*Double net* 20–1.

*Double taps* 15–8.

*Early doors* Early-morning exchanges between punters and bookmakers.

*Ear 'ole* 6–4 (from the tic-tac signal).

*Elef* 11–1.

*Elef a vier* 11–4.

*Enin* 9–1 ('nine' spelt backwards).

*Exes* 6–1.

*Face* 5–2 (tic-tac).

*Faces* Punters in the betting ring well known to the bookmakers as being well informed.

*Fiddlers* Bookmakers who will lay only small bets.

*Fivefold* A five-horse accumulator.

*Flimping* Giving under the odds; underpaying.

*Fourfold* A four-horse accumulator.

*Grand* £1,000.

*Hand* 5–1 (tic-tac).

*Hedging* Bookmakers reducing their liabilities by backing the horse themselves.

*Jolly* The favourite (the 'jolly old favourite').

*Kite* Cheque.

*Knock* Owe.

*Levels* Evens (variant: 'levels you devils!').

*Macaroni* 25–1.

*Monkey* £500.

*Nanny* The Tote ('nanny goat').

*Nap* A newspaper tipster's best bet of the day.

*Nelsons* Cash (Nelson Eddies . . . readies).

*Net* 10–1 ('ten' spelt backwards).

*Net and bice* 12–1.

*Net and rouf* 14–1.

*Net and ex* 16–1.

*Neves* 7–1 ('seven' spelt backwards).

*Not off* Said of a horse thought not to be trying to win.

*On the shoulders* 9–2.

*Over-broke* Betting with no profit margin (see page 59 above).

*Over-round* Betting with the margin in the bookie's favour (see page 58 above).

*Pony* £25, or 25–1.

*Rag* An outsider – a horse with no apparent chance.

*Rails bookmaker* One of a select group of racecourse bookmakers situated in the Tattersalls enclosure by the rail dividing that area from Members (where bookmakers are not usually allowed) – thus enabling members to bet from within their own enclosure.

*Rick* Error.

*Rock cake* Small bet.

*Rouf* 4–1 ('four' spelt backwards; pronounced 'rofe').

*Rule 4* Rule governing the effect on the market of a horse's being withdrawn just before the off: see page 76.

*Sais a ching* 6–5.

*Score* £20.

*Shoulder* 7–4 (tic-tac).

*Skinner* A horse unbacked – if he wins the bookmakers pay out nothing.

*Sky-rocket* Pocket.

*Sleeper* Uncollected winnings.

*Starting price* The price at which the horse is officially judged to have started the race.

*Steamer* A horse gambled on significantly on the morning of the race.

*Tank* Reserves of cash.

*T.H.* 8–1.

*Thick 'un* A big bet.

*Tic-tac* Sign language used on a racecourse by bookmakers to communicate with one another.

*Tips* 11–10 (tic-tac).

*Tissue* The course bookmakers' forecast of how the betting will open, prepared by a form expert employed by the bookies.

*Ton* £100.

*Top of the head* 9–4 (tic-tac).

*Up the arm* 11–8 (tic-tac).

*Village* The whole bookmaking fraternity.

*With the thumb* The price is being taken and won't last long (tic-tac).

*Wrist* 5–4 (tic-tac).

# Ready Reckoner

If you're using this, you've backed a winner. Or maybe you're working out what you would have won had the creature not fallen at the last – never a good idea. In either case, use the Ready Reckoner in this way:

Match your stake to the odds and read off the amount returned for a win bet or a place bet at one-quarter or one-fifth the odds.

Remember that *the returns include your original stake*, and that the figures in the Ready Reckoner do not include tax, which will be taken off your returns (not just your winnings) on off-course bets, unless you have bet 'tax paid'. Thus, 50p staked at 11–10 against returns £1.05 (55p winnings and 50p stake); 50p staked at 10–11 returns 95p (45p winnings and 50p stake). To find the return on a £1 each-way bet (a quarter the odds a place) at 6–1 you need to find the win element (£7.00) and add to it the place element (£2.50). Your returns are £9.50, of which £2 is your original stake.

Say you have a £1 double, and both horses win – at evens and 10–11. The first bet returns £2, which sum goes on to the second horse; when that one wins you end up with £3.82 – of which £1 is your original stake and £2.82 is your profit. For trebles, accumulators and more complex combination bets simply work through all the different individual stages.

## Evens

| Stake | Win | $^1/_5$ place return | $^1/_4$ place return |
|---|---|---|---|
| .01 | .02 | .01 | .01 |
| .02 | .04 | .02 | .02 |
| .03 | .06 | .04 | .04 |
| .04 | .08 | .05 | .05 |
| .05 | .10 | .06 | .06 |
| .10 | .20 | .12 | .12 |
| .20 | .40 | .24 | .25 |
| .30 | .60 | .36 | .37 |
| .40 | .80 | .48 | .50 |
| .50 | 1.00 | .60 | .62 |
| 1.00 | 2.00 | 1.20 | 1.25 |
| 2.00 | 4.00 | 2.40 | 2.50 |
| 5.00 | 10.00 | 6.00 | 6.25 |

| Win | ¹/₅ place return | ¹/₄ place return | Stake | Win | ¹/₅ place return | ¹/₄ place return |
|---|---|---|---|---|---|---|
| **11–10 against** | | | | | **11–10 on** | |
| .02 | .01 | .01 | .01 | .02 | .01 | .01 |
| .04 | .02 | .02 | .02 | .04 | .02 | .02 |
| .06 | .04 | .04 | .03 | .06 | .04 | .04 |
| .08 | .05 | .05 | .04 | .08 | .05 | .05 |
| .10 | .06 | .06 | .05 | .10 | .06 | .06 |
| .21 | .12 | .13 | .10 | .19 | .12 | .12 |
| .42 | .24 | .25 | .20 | .38 | .24 | .25 |
| .63 | .37 | .38 | .30 | .57 | .35 | .37 |
| .84 | .49 | .51 | .40 | .76 | .47 | .49 |
| 1.05 | .61 | .64 | .50 | .95 | .59 | .62 |
| 2.10 | 1.22 | 1.27 | 1.00 | 1.91 | 1.18 | 1.23 |
| 4.20 | 2.44 | 2.55 | 2.00 | 3.82 | 2.36 | 2.46 |
| 10.50 | 6.10 | 5.37 | 5.00 | 9.55 | 5.91 | 6.15 |
| **6–5 against** | | | | | **6–5 on** | |
| .02 | .01 | .01 | .01 | .02 | .01 | .01 |
| .04 | .02 | .03 | .02 | .04 | .02 | .02 |
| .07 | .04 | .04 | .03 | .05 | .03 | .04 |
| .09 | .05 | .05 | .04 | .07 | .05 | .05 |
| .11 | .06 | .06 | .05 | .09 | .06 | .06 |
| .22 | .12 | .13 | .10 | .18 | .12 | .12 |
| .44 | .25 | .26 | .20 | .37 | .23 | .24 |
| .66 | .37 | .39 | .30 | .55 | .35 | .36 |
| .88 | .50 | .52 | .40 | .73 | .46 | .48 |
| 1.10 | .62 | .65 | .50 | .92 | .58 | .60 |
| 2.20 | 1.24 | 1.30 | 1.00 | 1.83 | 1.17 | 1.21 |
| 4.40 | 2.48 | 2.60 | 2.00 | 3.67 | 2.33 | 2.42 |
| 11.00 | 6.20 | 6.50 | 5.00 | 9.17 | 5.83 | 6.05 |

| Win | ¹/₅ place return | ¹/₄ place return | Stake | Win | ¹/₅ place return | ¹/₄ place return |
|---|---|---|---|---|---|---|
| **5–4 against** | | | | | | **5–4 on** |
| .02 | .01 | .01 | .01 | .02 | .01 | .01 |
| .04 | .02 | .03 | .02 | .04 | .02 | .02 |
| .07 | .04 | .04 | .03 | .05 | .03 | .04 |
| .09 | .05 | .05 | .04 | .07 | .05 | .05 |
| .11 | .06 | .07 | .05 | .09 | .06 | .06 |
| .22 | .12 | .13 | .10 | .18 | .12 | .12 |
| .45 | .25 | .26 | .20 | .36 | .23 | .24 |
| .67 | .37 | .39 | .30 | .54 | .35 | .36 |
| .90 | .50 | .52 | .40 | .72 | .46 | .48 |
| 1.12 | .62 | .66 | .50 | .90 | .58 | .60 |
| 2.25 | 1.25 | 1.31 | 1.00 | 1.80 | 1.16 | 1.20 |
| 4.50 | 2.50 | 2.62 | 2.00 | 3.60 | 2.32 | 2.40 |
| 11.25 | 6.25 | 6.56 | 5.00 | 9.00 | 5.80 | 6.00 |
| **11–8 against** | | | | | | **11–8 on** |
| .02 | .01 | .01 | .01 | .02 | .01 | .01 |
| .05 | .03 | .03 | .02 | .03 | .02 | .02 |
| .07 | .04 | .04 | .03 | .05 | .03 | .04 |
| .09 | .05 | .05 | .04 | .07 | .05 | .05 |
| .12 | .06 | .07 | .05 | .09 | .06 | .06 |
| .24 | .13 | .13 | .10 | .17 | .11 | .12 |
| .47 | .25 | .27 | .20 | .35 | .23 | .24 |
| .71 | .38 | .40 | .30 | .52 | .34 | .35 |
| .95 | .51 | .54 | .40 | .69 | .46 | .47 |
| 1.19 | .64 | .67 | .50 | .86 | .57 | .59 |
| 2.37 | 1.27 | 1.34 | 1.00 | 1.73 | 1.15 | 1.18 |
| 4.75 | 2.55 | 2.68 | 2.00 | 3.45 | 2.29 | 2.36 |
| 11.87 | 6.37 | 6.71 | 5.00 | 8.64 | 5.73 | 5.91 |

| Win | ¹/₅ place return | ¹/₄ place return | Stake | Win | ¹/₅ place return | ¹/₄ place return |
|---|---|---|---|---|---|---|
| **6–4 against** | | | | | | **6–4 on** |
| .02 | .01 | .01 | .01 | .02 | .01 | .01 |
| .05 | .03 | .03 | .02 | .03 | .02 | .02 |
| .07 | .04 | .04 | .03 | .05 | .03 | .04 |
| .10 | .05 | .05 | .04 | .07 | .05 | .05 |
| .12 | .06 | .07 | .05 | .08 | .06 | .06 |
| .25 | .13 | .14 | .10 | .17 | .11 | .12 |
| .50 | .26 | .27 | .20 | .33 | .23 | .23 |
| .75 | .39 | .41 | .30 | .50 | .34 | .35 |
| 1.00 | .52 | .55 | .40 | .67 | .45 | .47 |
| 1.25 | .65 | .69 | .50 | .83 | .57 | .58 |
| 2.50 | 1.30 | 1.37 | 1.00 | 1.66 | 1.13 | 1.17 |
| 5.00 | 2.60 | 2.75 | 2.00 | 3.33 | 2.27 | 2.33 |
| 12.50 | 6.50 | 6.87 | 5.00 | 8.33 | 5.67 | 5.83 |
| **13–8 against** | | | | | | **13–8 on** |
| .03 | .01 | .01 | .01 | .02 | .01 | .01 |
| .05 | .03 | .03 | .02 | .03 | .02 | .02 |
| .08 | .04 | .04 | .03 | .05 | .03 | .03 |
| .10 | .05 | .06 | .04 | .06 | .04 | .05 |
| .13 | .07 | .07 | .05 | .08 | .06 | .06 |
| .26 | .13 | .14 | .10 | .16 | .11 | .12 |
| .52 | .26 | .28 | .20 | .32 | .22 | .23 |
| .79 | .40 | .42 | .30 | .48 | .34 | .35 |
| 1.05 | .53 | .56 | .40 | .65 | .45 | .46 |
| 1.31 | .66 | .70 | .50 | .81 | .56 | .58 |
| 2.62 | 1.32 | 1.40 | 1.00 | 1.62 | 1.11 | 1.15 |
| 5.25 | 2.65 | 2.81 | 2.00 | 3.23 | 2.25 | 2.31 |
| 13.12 | 6.62 | 7.03 | 5.00 | 8.08 | 5.62 | 5.77 |

| Win | 1/5 place return | 1/4 place return | Stake | Win | 1/5 place return | 1/4 place return |
|---|---|---|---|---|---|---|
| **7–4 against** | | | | | | **7–4 on** |
| .03 | .01 | .01 | .01 | .02 | .01 | .01 |
| .05 | .03 | .03 | .02 | .03 | .02 | .02 |
| .08 | .04 | .04 | .03 | .05 | .03 | .03 |
| .11 | .05 | .06 | .04 | .06 | .04 | .05 |
| .14 | .07 | .07 | .05 | .08 | .06 | .06 |
| .27 | .13 | .14 | .10 | .16 | .11 | .11 |
| .55 | .27 | .29 | .20 | .32 | .22 | .23 |
| .82 | .40 | .43 | .30 | .47 | .33 | .34 |
| 1.10 | .54 | .57 | .40 | .63 | .45 | .46 |
| 1.37 | .67 | .72 | .50 | .79 | .56 | .57 |
| 2.75 | 1.35 | 1.44 | 1.00 | 1.57 | 1.11 | 1.14 |
| 5.50 | 2.70 | 2.87 | 2.00 | 3.14 | 2.23 | 2.28 |
| 13.75 | 6.75 | 7.19 | 5.00 | 7.86 | 5.57 | 5.71 |
| **15–8 against** | | | | | | **15–8 on** |
| .03 | .01 | .01 | .01 | .02 | .01 | .01 |
| .06 | .03 | .03 | .02 | .03 | .02 | .02 |
| .09 | .04 | .04 | .03 | .05 | .03 | .03 |
| .11 | .05 | .06 | .04 | .06 | .04 | .05 |
| .14 | .07 | .07 | .05 | .08 | .06 | .06 |
| .29 | .13 | .14 | .10 | .15 | .11 | .11 |
| .57 | .27 | .29 | .20 | .31 | .22 | .23 |
| .86 | .41 | .44 | .30 | .46 | .33 | .34 |
| 1.15 | .55 | .59 | .40 | .61 | .44 | .45 |
| 1.44 | .69 | .73 | .50 | .77 | .55 | .57 |
| 2.87 | 1.37 | 1.47 | 1.00 | 1.53 | 1.11 | 1.13 |
| 5.75 | 2.75 | 2.94 | 2.00 | 3.07 | 2.21 | 2.26 |
| 14.37 | 6.87 | 7.34 | 5.00 | 7.67 | 5.53 | 5.67 |

| Win | $^1/_5$ place return | $^1/_4$ place return | Stake | Win | $^1/_5$ place return | $^1/_4$ place return |
|---|---|---|---|---|---|---|
| **2–1 against** | | | | | **2–1 on** | |
| .03 | .01 | .01 | .01 | .01 | .01 | .01 |
| .06 | .03 | .03 | .02 | .03 | .02 | .02 |
| .09 | .04 | .04 | .03 | .04 | .03 | .03 |
| .12 | .06 | .06 | .04 | .06 | .04 | .05 |
| .15 | .07 | .07 | .05 | .07 | .05 | .06 |
| .30 | .14 | .15 | .10 | .15 | .11 | .11 |
| .60 | .28 | .30 | .20 | .30 | .22 | .23 |
| .90 | .42 | .45 | .30 | .45 | .33 | .34 |
| 1.20 | .56 | .60 | .40 | .60 | .44 | .45 |
| 1.50 | .70 | .75 | .50 | .75 | .55 | .56 |
| 3.00 | 1.40 | 1.50 | 1.00 | 1.50 | 1.10 | 1.13 |
| 6.00 | 2.80 | 3.00 | 2.00 | 3.00 | 2.20 | 2.25 |
| 15.00 | 7.00 | 7.50 | 5.00 | 7.50 | 5.50 | 5.63 |
| **9–4 against** | | | | | **9–4 on** | |
| .03 | .01 | .02 | .01 | .01 | .01 | .02 |
| .06 | .03 | .03 | .02 | .03 | .02 | .02 |
| .10 | .04 | .05 | .03 | .04 | .03 | .03 |
| .13 | .06 | .06 | .04 | .06 | .04 | .04 |
| .16 | .07 | .08 | .05 | .07 | .05 | .06 |
| .32 | .14 | .16 | .10 | .14 | .11 | .11 |
| .65 | .29 | .31 | .20 | .29 | .22 | .22 |
| .97 | .43 | .47 | .30 | .43 | .33 | .33 |
| 1.30 | .58 | .62 | .40 | .58 | .44 | .44 |
| 1.62 | .72 | .78 | .50 | .72 | .54 | .56 |
| 3.25 | 1.45 | 1.56 | 1.00 | 1.44 | 1.09 | 1.11 |
| 6.50 | 2.90 | 3.11 | 2.00 | 2.89 | 2.18 | 2.22 |
| 16.25 | 7.25 | 7.81 | 5.00 | 7.22 | 5.44 | 5.56 |

| Win | ¹/₅ place return | ¹/₄ place return | Stake | Win | ¹/₅ place return | ¹/₄ place return |
|---|---|---|---|---|---|---|

## 5–2 against · 5–2 on

| Win | ¹/₅ place return | ¹/₄ place return | Stake | Win | ¹/₅ place return | ¹/₄ place return |
|---|---|---|---|---|---|---|
| .03 | .01 | .02 | .01 | .01 | .01 | .01 |
| .07 | .03 | .03 | .02 | .03 | .02 | .02 |
| .10 | .04 | .05 | .03 | .04 | .03 | .03 |
| .14 | .06 | .06 | .04 | .06 | .04 | .04 |
| .17 | .07 | .08 | .05 | .07 | .05 | .05 |
| .35 | .15 | .16 | .10 | .14 | .11 | .11 |
| .70 | .30 | .32 | .20 | .28 | .22 | .22 |
| 1.05 | .45 | .49 | .30 | .42 | .32 | .33 |
| 1.40 | .60 | .65 | .40 | .56 | .43 | .44 |
| 1.75 | .75 | .81 | .50 | .70 | .54 | .55 |
| 3.50 | 1.50 | 1.62 | 1.00 | 1.40 | 1.08 | 1.10 |
| 7.00 | 3.00 | 3.25 | 2.00 | 2.80 | 2.16 | 2.20 |
| 17.50 | 7.50 | 8.12 | 5.00 | 7.00 | 5.40 | 5.50 |

## 11–4 against · 11–4 on

| Win | ¹/₅ place return | ¹/₄ place return | Stake | Win | ¹/₅ place return | ¹/₄ place return |
|---|---|---|---|---|---|---|
| .04 | .02 | .02 | .01 | .01 | .01 | .01 |
| .07 | .03 | .03 | .02 | .03 | .02 | .02 |
| .11 | .05 | .05 | .03 | .04 | .03 | .03 |
| .15 | .06 | .07 | .04 | .05 | .04 | .04 |
| .19 | .08 | .08 | .05 | .07 | .05 | .05 |
| .37 | .16 | .17 | .10 | .14 | .11 | .11 |
| .75 | .31 | .34 | .20 | .27 | .21 | .22 |
| 1.12 | .46 | .51 | .30 | .41 | .32 | .33 |
| 1.50 | .62 | .67 | .40 | .55 | .43 | .44 |
| 1.87 | .77 | .84 | .50 | .68 | .54 | .55 |
| 3.75 | 1.55 | 1.69 | 1.00 | 1.36 | 1.07 | 1.08 |
| 7.50 | 3.10 | 3.37 | 2.00 | 2.73 | 2.14 | 2.18 |
| 18.75 | 7.75 | 8.44 | 5.00 | 6.82 | 5.36 | 5.45 |

| Win | ¹/₅ place return | ¹/₄ place return | Stake | Win | ¹/₅ place return | ¹/₄ place return |
|---|---|---|---|---|---|---|
| **3–1 against** | | | | | **3–1 on** | |
| .04 | .02 | .02 | .01 | .01 | .01 | .01 |
| .08 | .03 | .04 | .02 | .03 | .02 | .02 |
| .12 | .05 | .05 | .03 | .04 | .03 | .03 |
| .16 | .06 | .07 | .04 | .05 | .04 | .04 |
| .20 | .08 | .09 | .05 | .07 | .05 | .05 |
| .40 | .16 | .17 | .10 | .13 | .11 | .11 |
| .80 | .32 | .35 | .20 | .27 | .21 | .22 |
| 1.20 | .48 | .52 | .30 | .40 | .32 | .33 |
| 1.60 | .64 | .70 | .40 | .53 | .43 | .43 |
| 2.00 | .80 | .87 | .50 | .67 | .53 | .54 |
| 4.00 | 1.60 | 1.75 | 1.00 | 1.33 | 1.07 | 1.08 |
| 8.00 | 3.20 | 3.50 | 2.00 | 2.67 | 2.13 | 2.17 |
| 20.00 | 8.00 | 8.75 | 5.00 | 6.67 | 5.33 | 5.42 |
| **100–30 against** | | | | | **7–2 against** | |
| .04 | .02 | .02 | .01 | .04 | .02 | .02 |
| .09 | .03 | .04 | .02 | .09 | .03 | .04 |
| .13 | .05 | .05 | .03 | .13 | .05 | .06 |
| .17 | .07 | .07 | .04 | .18 | .07 | .07 |
| .22 | .08 | .09 | .05 | .22 | .08 | .09 |
| .43 | .17 | .18 | .10 | .45 | .17 | .19 |
| .87 | .33 | .37 | .20 | .90 | .34 | .37 |
| 1.30 | .50 | .55 | .30 | 1.35 | .51 | .56 |
| 1.73 | .67 | .73 | .40 | 1.80 | .68 | .75 |
| 2.17 | .83 | .92 | .50 | 2.25 | .85 | .94 |
| 4.33 | 1.67 | 1.83 | 1.00 | 4.50 | 1.70 | 1.87 |
| 8.67 | 3.33 | 3.67 | 2.00 | 9.00 | 3.40 | 3.75 |
| 21.67 | 8.33 | 9.17 | 5.00 | 22.50 | 8.50 | 9.37 |

| Win | $\frac{1}{5}$ place return | $\frac{1}{4}$ place return | Stake | Win | $\frac{1}{5}$ place return | $\frac{1}{4}$ place return |
|---|---|---|---|---|---|---|
| **4–1 against** | | | | **9–2 against** | | |
| .05 | .02 | .02 | .01 | .05 | .02 | .02 |
| .10 | .04 | .04 | .02 | .11 | .04 | .04 |
| .15 | .05 | .06 | .03 | .16 | .06 | .06 |
| .20 | .07 | .08 | .04 | .22 | .08 | .08 |
| .25 | .09 | .10 | .05 | .27 | .09 | .11 |
| .50 | .18 | .20 | .10 | .55 | .19 | .21 |
| 1.00 | .36 | .40 | .20 | 1.10 | .38 | .42 |
| 1.50 | .54 | .60 | .30 | 1.65 | .57 | .64 |
| 2.00 | .72 | .80 | .40 | 2.20 | .76 | .85 |
| 2.50 | .90 | 1.00 | .50 | 2.75 | .95 | 1.06 |
| 5.00 | 1.80 | 2.00 | 1.00 | 5.50 | 1.90 | 2.12 |
| 10.00 | 3.60 | 4.00 | 2.00 | 11.00 | 3.80 | 4.25 |
| 25.00 | 9.00 | 10.00 | 5.00 | 27.50 | 9.50 | 10.62 |
| **5–1 against** | | | | **11–2 against** | | |
| .06 | .02 | .02 | .01 | .06 | .02 | .02 |
| .12 | .04 | .04 | .02 | .13 | .04 | .05 |
| .18 | .06 | .07 | .03 | .19 | .06 | .07 |
| .24 | .08 | .09 | .04 | .26 | .08 | .09 |
| .30 | .10 | .11 | .05 | .32 | .10 | .12 |
| .60 | .20 | .22 | .10 | .65 | .21 | .24 |
| 1.20 | .40 | .45 | .20 | 1.30 | .42 | .48 |
| 1.80 | .60 | .67 | .30 | 1.95 | .63 | .71 |
| 2.40 | .80 | .90 | .40 | 2.60 | .84 | .95 |
| 3.00 | 1.00 | 1.12 | .50 | 3.25 | 1.05 | 1.19 |
| 6.00 | 2.00 | 2.25 | 1.00 | 6.50 | 2.10 | 2.38 |
| 12.00 | 4.00 | 4.50 | 2.00 | 13.00 | 4.20 | 4.75 |
| 30.00 | 10.00 | 11.25 | 5.00 | 32.50 | 10.50 | 11.87 |

| Win | ¹/₅ place return | ¹/₄ place return | Stake | Win | ¹/₅ place return | ¹/₄ place return |
|---|---|---|---|---|---|---|
| **6–1 against** | | | | **13–2 against** | | |
| .07 | .02 | .02 | .01 | .07 | .02 | .03 |
| .14 | .04 | .05 | .02 | .15 | .05 | .05 |
| .21 | .07 | .07 | .03 | .22 | .07 | .08 |
| .28 | .09 | .10 | .04 | .30 | .09 | .10 |
| .35 | .11 | .12 | .05 | .37 | .11 | .13 |
| .70 | .22 | .25 | .10 | .75 | .23 | .26 |
| 1.40 | .44 | .50 | .20 | 1.50 | .46 | .52 |
| 2.10 | .66 | .75 | .30 | 2.25 | .69 | .79 |
| 2.80 | .88 | 1.00 | .40 | 3.00 | .92 | 1.05 |
| 3.50 | 1.10 | 1.25 | .50 | 3.75 | 1.15 | 1.31 |
| 7.00 | 2.20 | 2.50 | 1.00 | 7.50 | 2.30 | 2.26 |
| 14.00 | 4.40 | 5.00 | 2.00 | 15.00 | 4.60 | 5.25 |
| 35.00 | 11.00 | 12.50 | 5.00 | 37.50 | 11.50 | 13.12 |
| **7–1 against** | | | | **15–2 against** | | |
| .08 | .02 | .03 | .01 | .08 | .02 | .03 |
| .16 | .05 | .05 | .02 | .17 | .05 | .06 |
| .24 | .07 | .08 | .03 | .25 | .07 | .09 |
| .32 | .10 | .11 | .04 | .34 | .10 | .11 |
| .40 | .12 | .14 | .05 | .42 | .12 | .14 |
| .80 | .24 | .27 | .10 | .85 | .25 | .29 |
| 1.60 | .48 | .55 | .20 | 1.70 | .50 | .57 |
| 2.40 | .72 | .82 | .30 | 2.55 | .75 | .86 |
| 3.20 | .96 | 1.10 | .40 | 3.40 | 1.00 | 1.15 |
| 4.00 | 1.20 | 1.37 | .50 | 4.25 | 1.25 | 1.44 |
| 8.00 | 2.40 | 2.75 | 1.00 | 8.50 | 2.50 | 2.87 |
| 16.00 | 4.80 | 5.50 | 2.00 | 17.00 | 5.00 | 5.75 |
| 40.00 | 12.00 | 13.75 | 5.00 | 42.50 | 12.50 | 14.37 |

| Win | ¹/₅ place return | ¹/₄ place return | Stake | Win | ¹/₅ place return | ¹/₄ place return |
|---|---|---|---|---|---|---|
| **8–1 against** | | | | **9–1 against** | | |
| .09 | .03 | .03 | .01 | .10 | .03 | .03 |
| .18 | .05 | .06 | .02 | .20 | .06 | .06 |
| .27 | .08 | .09 | .03 | .30 | .08 | .10 |
| .36 | .10 | .12 | .04 | .40 | .11 | .13 |
| .45 | .13 | .15 | .05 | .50 | .14 | .16 |
| .90 | .26 | .30 | .10 | 1.00 | .28 | .32 |
| 1.80 | .52 | .60 | .20 | 2.00 | .56 | .65 |
| 2.70 | .78 | .90 | .30 | 3.00 | .84 | .97 |
| 3.60 | 1.04 | 1.20 | .40 | 4.00 | 1.12 | 1.30 |
| 4.50 | 1.30 | 1.50 | .50 | 5.00 | 1.40 | 1.62 |
| 9.00 | 2.60 | 3.00 | 1.00 | 10.00 | 2.80 | 3.25 |
| 18.00 | 5.20 | 6.00 | 2.00 | 20.00 | 5.60 | 6.50 |
| 45.00 | 13.00 | 15.00 | 5.00 | 50.00 | 14.00 | 16.25 |
| **10–1 against** | | | | **11–1 against** | | |
| .11 | .03 | .03 | .01 | .12 | .03 | .04 |
| .22 | .06 | .07 | .02 | .24 | .06 | .07 |
| .33 | .09 | .10 | .03 | .36 | .10 | .11 |
| .44 | .12 | .14 | .04 | .48 | .13 | .15 |
| .55 | .15 | .17 | .05 | .60 | .16 | .19 |
| 1.10 | .30 | .35 | .10 | 1.20 | .32 | .37 |
| 2.20 | .60 | .70 | .20 | 2.40 | .64 | .75 |
| 3.30 | .90 | 1.05 | .30 | 3.60 | .96 | 1.12 |
| 4.40 | 1.20 | 1.40 | .40 | 4.80 | 1.28 | 1.50 |
| 5.50 | 1.50 | 1.75 | .50 | 6.00 | 1.60 | 1.87 |
| 11.00 | 3.00 | 3.50 | 1.00 | 12.00 | 3.20 | 3.75 |
| 22.00 | 6.00 | 7.00 | 2.00 | 24.00 | 6.40 | 7.50 |
| 55.00 | 15.00 | 17.50 | 5.00 | 60.00 | 16.00 | 18.75 |

| Win | 1/5 place return | 1/4 place return | Stake | Win | 1/5 place return | 1/4 place return |
|---|---|---|---|---|---|---|

**12–1 against**             **14–1 against**

| Win | 1/5 place return | 1/4 place return | Stake | Win | 1/5 place return | 1/4 place return |
|---|---|---|---|---|---|---|
| .13 | .03 | .04 | .01 | .15 | .04 | .04 |
| .26 | .07 | .08 | .02 | .30 | .08 | .09 |
| .39 | .10 | .12 | .03 | .45 | .11 | .13 |
| .52 | .14 | .16 | .04 | .60 | .15 | .18 |
| .65 | .17 | .20 | .05 | .75 | .19 | .22 |
| 1.30 | .34 | .40 | .10 | 1.50 | .38 | .45 |
| 2.60 | .68 | .80 | .20 | 3.00 | .76 | .90 |
| 3.90 | 1.02 | 1.20 | .30 | 4.50 | 1.14 | 1.35 |
| 5.20 | 1.36 | 1.60 | .40 | 6.00 | 1.52 | 1.80 |
| 6.50 | 1.70 | 2.00 | .50 | 7.50 | 1.90 | 2.25 |
| 13.00 | 3.40 | 4.00 | 1.00 | 15.00 | 3.80 | 4.50 |
| 26.00 | 6.80 | 8.00 | 2.00 | 30.00 | 7.60 | 9.00 |
| 65.00 | 17.00 | 20.00 | 5.00 | 75.00 | 19.00 | 22.50 |

**16–1 against**             **20–1 against**

| Win | 1/5 place return | 1/4 place return | Stake | Win | 1/5 place return | 1/4 place return |
|---|---|---|---|---|---|---|
| .17 | .04 | .05 | .01 | .21 | .05 | .06 |
| .34 | .08 | .10 | .02 | .42 | .10 | .12 |
| .51 | .13 | .15 | .03 | .63 | .15 | .18 |
| .68 | .17 | .20 | .04 | .84 | .20 | .24 |
| .85 | .21 | .25 | .05 | 1.05 | .25 | .30 |
| 1.70 | .42 | .50 | .10 | 2.10 | .50 | .60 |
| 3.40 | .84 | 1.00 | .20 | 4.20 | 1.00 | 1.20 |
| 5.10 | 1.26 | 1.50 | .30 | 6.30 | 1.50 | 1.80 |
| 6.80 | 1.68 | 2.00 | .40 | 8.40 | 2.00 | 2.40 |
| 8.50 | 2.10 | 2.50 | .50 | 10.50 | 2.50 | 3.00 |
| 17.00 | 4.20 | 5.00 | 1.00 | 21.00 | 5.00 | 6.00 |
| 34.00 | 8.40 | 10.00 | 2.00 | 42.00 | 10.00 | 12.00 |
| 85.00 | 21.00 | 25.00 | 5.00 | 105.00 | 25.00 | 30.00 |

| Win | ¹/₅ place return | ¹/₄ place return | Stake | Win | ¹/₅ place return | ¹/₄ place return |
|---|---|---|---|---|---|---|
| **25–1 against** | | | | **33–1 against** | | |
| .26 | .06 | .07 | .01 | .34 | .08 | .09 |
| .52 | .12 | .14 | .02 | .68 | .15 | .18 |
| .78 | .18 | .22 | .03 | 1.02 | .23 | .28 |
| 1.04 | .24 | .29 | .04 | 1.36 | .30 | .37 |
| 1.30 | .30 | .36 | .05 | 1.70 | .38 | .46 |
| 2.60 | .60 | .72 | .10 | 3.40 | .76 | .92 |
| 5.20 | 1.20 | 1.45 | .20 | 6.80 | 1.52 | 1.85 |
| 7.80 | 1.80 | 2.17 | .30 | 10.20 | 2.28 | 2.77 |
| 10.40 | 2.40 | 2.90 | .40 | 13.60 | 3.04 | 3.70 |
| 13.00 | 3.00 | 3.62 | .50 | 17.00 | 3.80 | 4.62 |
| 26.00 | 6.00 | 7.25 | 1.00 | 34.00 | 7.60 | 9.25 |
| 52.00 | 12.00 | 14.50 | 2.00 | 68.00 | 15.20 | 18.50 |
| 130.00 | 30.00 | 36.25 | 5.00 | 170.00 | 38.00 | 46.25 |
| **50–1 against** | | | | **66–1 against** | | |
| .51 | .11 | .14 | .01 | .67 | .14 | .18 |
| 1.02 | .22 | .27 | .02 | 1.34 | .28 | .35 |
| 1.53 | .33 | .41 | .03 | 2.01 | .43 | .53 |
| 2.04 | .44 | .54 | .04 | 2.68 | .57 | .70 |
| 2.55 | .55 | .68 | .05 | 3.35 | .71 | .88 |
| 5.10 | 1.10 | 1.35 | .10 | 6.70 | 1.42 | 1.75 |
| 10.20 | 2.20 | 2.70 | .20 | 13.40 | 2.84 | 3.50 |
| 15.30 | 3.30 | 4.05 | .30 | 20.10 | 4.26 | 5.25 |
| 20.40 | 4.40 | 5.40 | .40 | 26.80 | 5.68 | 7.00 |
| 25.50 | 5.50 | 6.75 | .50 | 33.50 | 7.10 | 8.75 |
| 51.00 | 11.00 | 13.50 | 1.00 | 67.00 | 14.20 | 17.50 |
| 102.00 | 22.00 | 27.00 | 2.00 | 134.00 | 28.40 | 35.00 |
| 255.00 | 55.00 | 67.50 | 5.00 | 335.00 | 71.00 | 87.50 |

# Weight-for-Age Scales

**Flat**

The scale shows the number of pounds by which it is deemed the average horse in each age group falls short of maturity at different dates and distances.

| Dist. (flgs) | Age | Jan. 1–15 | Jan. 16–31 | Feb. 1–14 | Feb. 15–29 | March 1–15 | March 16–31 | April 1–15 | April 16–30 | May 1–15 | May 16–31 |
|---|---|---|---|---|---|---|---|---|---|---|---|
| 5 | 2 | – | – | – | – | – | 47 | 44 | 41 | 38 | 36 |
|   | 3 | 15 | 15 | 14 | 14 | 13 | 12 | 11 | 10 | 9 | 8 |
| 6 | 2 | – | – | – | – | – | – | – | – | 44 | 41 |
|   | 3 | 16 | 16 | 15 | 15 | 14 | 13 | 12 | 11 | 10 | 9 |
| 7 | 2 | – | – | – | – | – | – | – | – | – | – |
|   | 3 | 18 | 18 | 17 | 17 | 16 | 15 | 14 | 13 | 12 | 11 |
| 8 | 2 | – | – | – | – | – | – | – | – | – | – |
|   | 3 | 20 | 20 | 19 | 19 | 18 | 17 | 15 | 14 | 13 | 12 |
| 9 | 3 | 22 | 22 | 21 | 21 | 20 | 19 | 17 | 15 | 14 | 13 |
|   | 4 | 1 | 1 | – | – | – | – | – | – | – | – |
| 10 | 3 | 23 | 23 | 22 | 22 | 21 | 20 | 19 | 17 | 15 | 14 |
|   | 4 | 2 | 2 | 1 | 1 | – | – | – | – | – | – |
| 11 | 3 | 24 | 24 | 23 | 23 | 22 | 21 | 20 | 19 | 17 | 15 |
|   | 4 | 3 | 3 | 2 | 2 | 1 | 1 | – | – | – | – |
| 12 | 3 | 25 | 25 | 24 | 24 | 23 | 22 | 21 | 20 | 19 | 17 |
|   | 4 | 4 | 4 | 3 | 3 | 2 | 2 | 1 | 1 | – | – |
| 13 | 3 | 26 | 26 | 25 | 25 | 24 | 23 | 22 | 21 | 20 | 19 |
|   | 4 | 5 | 5 | 4 | 4 | 3 | 3 | 2 | 1 | – | – |
| 14 | 3 | 27 | 27 | 26 | 26 | 25 | 24 | 23 | 22 | 21 | 20 |
|   | 4 | 6 | 6 | 5 | 5 | 4 | 4 | 3 | 2 | 1 | – |
| 15 | 3 | 28 | 28 | 27 | 27 | 26 | 25 | 24 | 23 | 22 | 21 |
|   | 4 | 6 | 6 | 5 | 5 | 4 | 4 | 3 | 3 | 2 | 1 |
| 16 | 3 | 29 | 29 | 28 | 28 | 27 | 26 | 25 | 24 | 23 | 22 |
|   | 4 | 7 | 7 | 6 | 6 | 5 | 5 | 4 | 4 | 3 | 2 |
| 18 | 3 | 31 | 31 | 30 | 30 | 29 | 28 | 27 | 26 | 25 | 24 |
|   | 4 | 8 | 8 | 7 | 7 | 6 | 6 | 5 | 5 | 4 | 3 |
| 20 | 3 | 33 | 33 | 32 | 32 | 31 | 30 | 29 | 28 | 27 | 26 |
|   | 4 | 9 | 9 | 8 | 8 | 7 | 7 | 6 | 6 | 5 | 4 |

| June 1–15 | 16–30 | July 1–15 | 16–31 | Aug. 1–15 | 16–31 | Sept. 1–15 | 16–30 | Oct. 1–15 | 16–31 | Nov. 1–15 | 16–30 | Dec. 1–15 | 16–31 |
|---|---|---|---|---|---|---|---|---|---|---|---|---|---|
| 34 | 32 | 30 | 28 | 26 | 24 | 22 | 20 | 19 | 18 | 17 | 17 | 16 | 16 |
| 7 | 6 | 5 | 4 | 3 | 2 | 1 | 1 | – | – | – | – | – | – |
| 38 | 36 | 33 | 31 | 28 | 26 | 24 | 22 | 21 | 20 | 19 | 18 | 17 | 17 |
| 8 | 7 | 6 | 5 | 4 | 3 | 2 | 2 | 2 | 1 | 1 | – | – | – |
| – | – | 38 | 35 | 32 | 30 | 27 | 25 | 23 | 22 | 21 | 20 | 19 | 19 |
| 10 | 9 | 8 | 7 | 6 | 5 | 4 | 3 | 2 | 2 | 1 | 1 | – | – |
| – | – | – | – | 37 | 34 | 31 | 28 | 26 | 24 | 23 | 22 | 21 | 20 |
| 11 | 10 | 9 | 8 | 7 | 6 | 5 | 4 | 3 | 3 | 2 | 2 | 1 | 1 |
| 12 | 11 | 10 | 9 | 8 | 7 | 6 | 5 | 4 | 4 | 3 | 3 | 2 | 2 |
| – | – | – | – | – | – | – | – | – | – | – | – | – | – |
| 13 | 12 | 11 | 10 | 9 | 8 | 7 | 6 | 5 | 5 | 4 | 4 | 3 | 3 |
| – | – | – | – | – | – | – | – | – | – | – | – | – | – |
| 14 | 13 | 12 | 11 | 10 | 9 | 8 | 7 | 6 | 6 | 5 | 5 | 4 | 4 |
| – | – | – | – | – | – | – | – | – | – | – | – | – | – |
| 15 | 14 | 13 | 12 | 11 | 10 | 9 | 8 | 7 | 7 | 6 | 6 | 5 | 5 |
| – | – | – | – | – | – | – | – | – | – | – | – | – | – |
| 17 | 15 | 14 | 13 | 12 | 11 | 10 | 9 | 8 | 8 | 7 | 7 | 6 | 6 |
| – | – | – | – | – | – | – | – | – | – | – | – | – | – |
| 19 | 17 | 15 | 14 | 13 | 12 | 11 | 10 | 9 | 9 | 8 | 8 | 7 | 7 |
| – | – | – | – | – | – | – | – | – | – | – | – | – | – |
| 20 | 19 | 17 | 15 | 14 | 13 | 12 | 11 | 10 | 9 | 8 | 8 | 7 | 7 |
| – | – | – | – | – | – | – | – | – | – | – | – | – | – |
| 21 | 20 | 19 | 17 | 15 | 14 | 13 | 12 | 11 | 10 | 9 | 9 | 8 | 8 |
| 1 | – | – | – | – | – | – | – | – | – | – | – | – | – |
| 23 | 22 | 21 | 20 | 18 | 16 | 14 | 13 | 12 | 11 | 10 | 10 | 9 | 9 |
| 2 | 1 | – | – | – | – | – | – | – | – | – | – | – | – |
| 25 | 24 | 23 | 22 | 20 | 18 | 16 | 14 | 13 | 12 | 11 | 11 | 10 | 10 |
| 3 | 2 | 1 | – | – | – | – | – | – | – | – | – | – | – |

## Jumping

The scale shows the weight allowances, in pounds, which three-year-olds and four-year-olds will receive from horses aged five and upwards in hurdle races, and which four-year-olds and five-year-olds will receive from horses aged six and upwards in steeplechases.

### Hurdle races

| Dist. (m) | Age | Jan. | Feb. | March | April | May | June |
|---|---|---|---|---|---|---|---|
| 2 | 3 | – | – | – | – | – | – |
|  | 4 | 12 | 10 | 8 | 6 | 5 | 5 |
| 2½ | 3 | – | – | – | – | – | – |
|  | 4 | 13 | 11 | 9 | 7 | 6 | 6 |
| 3 | 3 | – | – | – | – | – | – |
|  | 4 | 14 | 12 | 10 | 8 | 7 | 7 |

### Steeplechases

| Dist. (m) | Age | Jan. | Feb. | March | April | May | June |
|---|---|---|---|---|---|---|---|
| 2 | 4 | – | – | – | – | – | – |
|  | 5 | 10 | 9 | 8 | 7 | 6 | 6 |
| 2½ | 4 | – | – | – | – | – | – |
|  | 5 | 11 | 10 | 9 | 8 | 7 | 7 |
| 3 | 4 | – | – | – | – | – | – |
|  | 5 | 12 | 11 | 10 | 9 | 8 | 8 |

| July | Aug. | Sept. | Oct. | Nov. | Dec. |
|------|------|-------|------|------|------|
| 20 | 20 | 18 | 17 | 16 | 14 |
| 3 | 3 | 2 | 1 | – | – |
| 21 | 21 | 19 | 18 | 17 | 15 |
| 3 | 3 | 2 | 1 | – | – |
| 23 | 23 | 21 | 19 | 18 | 16 |
| 4 | 4 | 3 | 2 | 1 | – |

| July | Aug. | Sept. | Oct. | Nov. | Dec. |
|------|------|-------|------|------|------|
| 15 | 15 | 14 | 13 | 12 | 11 |
| 3 | 3 | 2 | 1 | – | – |
| 16 | 16 | 15 | 14 | 13 | 12 |
| 4 | 4 | 3 | 2 | 1 | – |
| 17 | 17 | 16 | 15 | 14 | 13 |
| 5 | 5 | 4 | 3 | 2 | 1 |

# Index